$\mathcal{P}$ h o e n i x

— f r o m   t h e —

$\mathcal{A}$ s h e s

Deb Childs

Phoenix

from the

Ashes

Rebuilding Shattered Lives

Saul Levine, M.D.

KEY PORTER BOOKS

To the reader: To protect the identities of the individuals whom I know very well or whom I have worked with, the histories in this book are fictionalized. In addition, many are amalgams of individuals who exhibit similar patterns.

Canadian Cataloguing in Publication Data

Levine, Saul, 1938-
  Phoenix from the ashes

ISBN 1-55013-282-2

1. Self-respect.   I. Title.

BF697.5.S46L4 1992   158'.1   C90-095354-3

Key Porter Books Limited
70 The Esplanade
Toronto, Ontario
Canada M5E 1R2

Typesetting: Computer Composition of Canada Inc.

Printed and bound in Canada

92 93 94 95 96 6 5 4 3 2 1

Contents

L'Chaim

To Life

Foreword

HUMAN BEHAVIOR SEEMS TO FOLLOW A LINE that is evolutionary rather than revolutionary. It would appear — and this is good news indeed — that seeds of wellness are planted in everyone at the same time as those virulent seeds that produce self-hatred and profound aloneness. Saul Levine, one of Canada's most respected psychiatrists, believes that when people reach a catastrophic moment in their lives and are closest to suicide, they are also at a springing-up place.

It happened to him, as he is honest and brave enough to say. It happened to nine others described in this book: overachievers, incest survivors, alcoholics, the young, the middle-aged, the old. In the darkest night of their souls, they turned adversity into a triumph of the spirit.

He writes that there are three essentials for inner survival: self-esteem, belonging, believing. He speaks of finding one's "inner home" and he gently supports the concept of a spiritual quest. Wallace Stevens, the American poet, once pointed out that the major poetic idea in the world has always been the idea of God. The wounded among us, and who is without a wound?, seek the divinity of magical healing.

The remedy is not in our stars, to paraphrase Shakespeare, but in ourselves. I find that wisdom both ennobling and a great comfort. This is a wonderful book, full of the joyful experiences of people who grew themselves. Thank you Saul.

June Callwood

Preface

IN THIS BOOK, YOU WILL MEET NINE MEN AND women of all ages who experience crisis, survive, and go on to lead more meaningful, happier lives. Judging strictly from appearances, none of them would seem to be destined for personal disaster of any kind. They were all raised in two-parent, middle-class households. Their crises don't involve wars or famine or disease. Yet their despair and sense of futility about life are not any less real because of this, nor their courage in turning their lives around any less inspiring.

There is a story behind the title of this book: *Phoenix from the Ashes*. According to ancient Egyptian mythology, the phoenix was a magnificent bird, but it was overly impressed with its own beauty and power. Convinced of its invincibility, this wondrous creature flew too close to the powerful rays of the sun and was burned to a pile of ashes. That same sun then sent rays of healing warmth to those ashes, and from that emanated a resurrected bird, even more magnificent, but certainly more humble, than before. As our stories unfold, the message of this mythical parable will be revealed.

I have been uneasy for a long time with the traditional psychiatric approach to people's problems. Generally, a diagnosis of illness is made, followed by an attempt to "cure" the "sick personality." In professional schools, much is taught about psychopathology but very little about normalcy and health. The approach to emotional problems and solutions in this book is quite different. Although the cases are based on people who obviously have personal difficulties of one sort or another, the individuals are essentially healthy. What happens to them is a result of a confluence of personality problems and circumstances that could befall any of us.

As a psychiatrist, I have had the privilege to meet hundreds of people in emotionally close encounters and have been able to learn much about our common struggles, pleasures, pains, and conundrums. In addition, whenever I have had the opportunity, I have visited temples, churches, synagogues, ashrams, mosques, and other houses of worship around the world. In mood, hopes, and reverence, their similarities far outweigh their differences. I have also studied many people in so-called cults, new belief systems, and Born Again and New Age religions and groups. It is strikingly clear that we are all searching for inner peace, for a sense of acceptance, and for a rationale to our lives. I am a Jewish man who subscribes to the Hindu and Buddhist view of karma — a kind of inner, personal energy capable of correcting one's destiny; to the Protestant perception of providence — a combination of hopeful expectation and God; and to the ecumenical concept of a human community. I have discovered that, to the extent that we achieve acceptance of and peace within ourselves (self-esteem), fulfilling relationships with others (belonging), and a meaningful value system (belief), these three factors will ultimately be the measure of our lives. How we accomplish this, even under the most trying conditions, is the subject of this book.

I collect eggs. My collection, consisting of approximately 160 eggs from more than sixty countries, serves as a constant reminder to me of love, beauty, and spirituality. The exquisite shape of the egg has been adopted by many cultures and religions as a symbol of regeneration, the life cycle, generativity, and spirituality. It represents the harmonious unity of mind, body, and soul, and it signifies to me the life-force God has bestowed on us, which enables us to overcome our darkest hours.

Acknowledgments

THERE ARE MANY PEOPLE WHO HAVE HELPED ME personally, enabling me to write this book and, more importantly, supporting me in turning my own life around.

First and foremost are my patients, friends, and others who taught me so much about losses, life, and love, and whose setbacks, struggles, and successes have inspired me.

I owe so much gratitude to *ma belle Canadienne*, Isabelle Coté, whose support, encouragement, and love have elevated my spirits; and to Kathy Wilcox, who changed my life.

To my dear sons, Jaime, Mischa, and Zachary, and to their mother, Ellie, with whom I shared so much; to my parents, Mike and Bess; to my sister, Joyce Morrison, and her husband, Ken; to the Levine descendants from Kamai and Vilna, now in Canada and Israel; to Berl and Gissa Schiff, Ron and Yvonne Singer, Moses Znaimer and Marilyn Lightstone; to Rabbi Reuven Slonim; to Rosie and Itchy Abella; to Liz Manson, Diane Sacks and Marie-Claude Lemieux; to Murray and Barbara Frum, Terry and Laurie Sullivan, Peter and Annette Ellis, David and Honey Lippman, Patsy and

Tony Doob, Joan and Peter Moss, Sandy and Paul Druckman, Myrna and David Ichelson; to Hazel Ipp, Norma Kent, Marian Osterweiss, Janet Yorston, Denise Howe, Elaine Smith, and Sally Julien; to Yasin and Barbara Balbaky, Alycia and Frank Markel, Marvin and Estherkeh Tile, Mark and Corin Greenberg, Raziel and Jeanne Gershater, Seymour and Terri Silverberg; to Adrienne Clarkson, and John Ralston Saul; to Amiram and Rika Gonen, and Fred and Maureen Glaser; to Richard Uren, Lew and Pat Judd, David Weisstub, Michael Levine, Sholom Glouberman, George Awad, Fuller Torrey, Gordon Winocur; to Sanjay, Dyppak, Latha, and Ram Ramachandran; to Chryssie Rejman, Linda Bainbridge, Carolyn Jones, Marilyn Dennis, Shirley Malanych, Bernice Krafchick and Dini Petty; to Linda Dranoff and June Clarke; to Michael Rosenbluth, Ken Shulman, Dan Roncari, Martin Barkin, Harry Shulman, Paul Garfinkel, Morty Mamelak, Ralph Pohlman, Robert Cleghorn, Ron Billings, and the late Jack Holmes; to Sarah Swartz, Nicole Stewart, Merlyn Arthur, Cynthia Martin and Lissa Smith; To all of you I say, thank you.

To Tony Bombini, whose place on Georgian Bay allowed me to write and heal; to Rose Shakato and the rest of the staff at the wondrous Leighton Art Colony at the Banff Centre; and to Fanny Silberman, whose cottage, food, love, food, advice, and food, nurtured me: I am very grateful.

A special thank you also to Jinks Hoffman, who helped me so much in my spiritual quest. To Roz Ward, my secretary, who was invaluable, both personally and professionally; to Sara Stein who reviewed the first draft, and who encouraged the second; and to Anna Porter, my publisher, who cajoled me; to Phyllis Bruce, Key Porter's vice-president and senior editor, who nursed me along, never giving up on me; to Laurie Coulter, without whose help there would simply be no book; and to my superb editor, Meg Taylor, who also collects eggs, and is a kindred spirit.

Finally, to many others of my colleagues and friends at Sunnybrook Health Science Centre, The University of Toronto, CITY-TV, the Toronto *Star*, Youthdale and elsewhere, who tolerated my *mishugass*, and kept the faith, I send vibes of heartfelt appreciation.

If I do not do for myself, who will do it for me?
If I care only for myself, what am I?
And if not now, when?
—*Pirkei Avot, 1:14*

1. Self-esteem, Belonging, and Believing

TODAY, WHILE WORKING ON THIS BOOK, I NOTICED that a postcard I had received yesterday and a letter from what seems a very long time ago were lying side by side on the desk. Two lines from the letter could be read from where I sat — "I hope that you find it within your heart to forgive me. I just couldn't live with my intense pain any longer, and continue to inflict others with it" — and two lines from the postcard — "Dear Dr. Levine: Thanks to you I am able to again appreciate what the world has to offer. Greetings from Florida. Matthew."

The lines from my own suicide note may resemble lines you yourself have written or have thought about writing, or you may recognize them as words you imagine someone you care about might write. I read those brief sentences now and feel pulled into the old pain. Its familiarity upsets me, reminding me of another place, another time, another me. Then I read Matthew's words, the pain lifts and I rejoice.

When I first met Matthew, he was lying under a hospital bed trying to starve himself to death. He had been in a terrible boating accident five years earlier at sixteen, and had lost areas of his intelligence, his ability to do simple arithmetic, his girlfriend, the works. My hand happened to be the one he took hold of in his time of crisis. It just as easily could have been the hand of a psychologist, social worker, nurse, a member of the clergy, a friend — any number of people. Twice a week I helped him work his way along a path that was too rocky and steep at times for him to follow alone. Because of the complexity of his problems, he also worked with a number of other professionals. The rest of the time, he struggled along on his own, sometimes slipping back in despair, sometimes making great strides. Today he lives in an apartment with two other young men, attends college, and has a part-time job. He has completely rebuilt his life.

These two pieces of paper represent opposite ends of a journey. It may seem too far to travel from the bleakness of one to the thanksgiving of the other, but I am writing to tell you that it is possible.

The Emotional Foundations of Our Lives

Much of my professional life has been spent studying young people who have left home to join radical groups, or "cults," as the popular media call them. Contrary to what most people believe, these children were from warm, concerned homes that had provided all the material, intellectual, and social benefits thought to ensure happiness. For them to make these radical departures, it was obvious something was missing from their young lives, something that the groups they joined provided. I found that all the radical groups I studied — from the Moonies to the Healthy Happy Holy Organization — gave their members three essentials for inner survival: self-esteem, belonging, and believing.

These kids felt terrific about themselves, their group, and their belief system.

In addition to the basics of life that we need to survive — food, water, shelter, and clothing — we need these three intangibles to nurture our souls. Together they form the foundation blocks of our inner homes. One or two may predominate, but we need to find all three in our quest for a rewarding life and for a successful recovery from major losses.

I like to think of self-esteem as the care we take of our inner homes. It is the respect and caring we have for ourselves in spite of our deficiencies. How we view ourselves is a crucial determinant in how we feel about our relationships, work, indeed, our entire lives. Even if we suffer from low self-esteem, each of us has within us a core of basic self-respect that can be tapped to give the resilience we need to survive serious difficulties.

Belonging is our sense of community with others or our need for affiliation with others. We all want to be loved, to be understood by family and friends. Most of us long for a compatible partner with whom we can share our lives. We also need a wider community of people in which we feel accepted and appreciated. Together this makes up our sense of belonging. Without it, we feel alienated from the world.

Believing is being at home in the universe or the need to have a system of values to give meaning to our lives. It can be spiritual or religious in nature or it can be based on social, political, or personal ideologies. It is what helps guide our actions and formulate our goals. Without a belief system, there is a big void in our lives.

Life would no doubt be easier if we were all given a large dollop of self-esteem, belonging, and believing before we entered this world. Unfortunately, we aren't, and what in fact determines our personalities is complex. The genes and chromosomes we have inherited from our parents give us different physical, emotional, and intellectual characteristics. Outside influences — relationships with our family, our physical surroundings, the state of our health — also play an important role in shaping us. What we do share, though, are our vulnerabilities and fears.

Unless we know people very well, most of us look at other people and draw conclusions about their lives from their appearance and visible behavior, their life style, and the messages they want to give us. Few of us really know what is going on in the hearts and minds of even our closest friends. If we did, we would know that we all have questions about our own self-worth, our accomplishments, and our purpose in life. At some point, we all worry about our relationships and the emptiness inside we experience from time to time. But when we have these feelings, many of us feel alone, as though our questions were unique to us. At these times, we need to know that other people understand our fears. Yet when we most need to feel a sense of affiliation with others, we are usually isolated and unable to connect. This sense of isolation is usually a secret state we keep inside ourselves and rarely examine unless we must.

If we feel generally good about ourselves, have a number of supportive people in our lives, and have some sense of purpose, we can overcome those intermittent feelings of isolation and emptiness. We learn to emphasize the successes and rewarding relationships we have. On the other hand, if the positive attributes of our lives are insufficient or lacking altogether, it becomes increasingly difficult to maintain appearances and to continue functioning in a responsible, productive, caring manner. "Appearances" are just that — a positive facade. Sometimes they may be an accurate reflection of feelings, but at other times they are unsuccessful attempts at burying reality. It's very difficult to maintain a positive facade if underneath you are feeling empty or in pain.

Maintaining appearances is often tied in with our personal beliefs or myths about ourselves. These myths are coping mechanisms, which enable us to play a role that feels comfortable or familiar. Classical psychoanalytic theory uses the term "defense mechanisms" to describe unconscious (out of our awareness) behaviors designed to keep hidden conflicts buried and to reduce anxiety. I'm not referring to these, but to beliefs about ourselves that we know are invalid or flawed, yet which we continue to pursue with a kind of perverse dedication. These very conscious personal myths may take the form of "I am a loser," or "I am bad," or "I have to protect everyone in my family," or "Everyone is against me," or "I must achieve great success." I'm sure you could add a few of your own to the list.

The label I hung around my own neck for years was "not good enough." The more success I had, the more I doubted my real abilities. As a high-school student, I felt I was pulling the wool over the teachers' eyes or was extraordinarily lucky. I didn't believe my successes. Now, when I say to troubled men and women who outwardly appear to be very successful, "Even when you achieve great success, I bet you don't feel like you deserve it. I bet you feel like a fraud," they look surprised. "How do you know that?" they ask. It's simply because I've been there, and I've met many people who share a similar myth about themselves.

The problem with believing these myths is that they often become self-fulfilling prophecies and can lead to painful and precarious situations. Many of these coping mechanisms and behaviors appear to be effective in the short run, but can become destructive in the long run if they are not confronted, contained, and changed. For example, if you believe you are incompetent at everything you do, you may cover up your low self-esteem by becoming a workaholic. Your relationships with other people may be adversely affected, which will in turn place your sense of belonging in jeopardy. In some cases, the myth is not covered up, but enacted. If you are convinced that everyone is against you, for instance, you may set up situations that will result in someone rejecting you.

You probably have a good idea of what your own personal myths are. I ask people when they first come to see me to write out a list of everything they admire and respect about themselves — physically, emotionally, and cognitively. Then I ask them to do the opposite, to list everything they hate about themselves. I ask them not to include what other people have told them, but what they truly think about themselves. Invariably, the list of negatives far outweighs the list of positives. The emotional foundations of their lives are shaky at best, and nearly nonexistent at worst.

Traditional psychiatric theory would look for someone to blame for these shaky foundations. Parents are a good bet. Recently I talked with a young teen-age boy who had been admitted to a group treatment home after his arrest. Throughout his life, his mother had repeatedly called him "a fucking jerk-off," which, of course, had led him to believe that he should behave like one. He went to school sporadically and spent the rest of the time "hanging out" or shoplifting. Throughout his childhood and adolescence, he wondered why a mother would say such brutal things to her son. She died before he had a chance to ask her, leaving him with many conflicting feelings. He had imagined killing her, the source of his misery, on numerous occasions, so when she did die, he felt responsible for her death. Remorse, relief, and sadness at her passing have combined to make a mixed-up kid even more miserable with his lot in life. His poetry, which is full of images of suicide interspersed with hostile thoughts about his mother, reflects emotions that are constantly at or near the boiling point.

It would be easy to blame all of this boy's horrendous problems on his dysfunctional family. Parents play a major role in determining how their children turn out. When they don't give their sons and daughters love, respect, and encouragement, their children's emotional foundations will be weakened. If this is the case, learning more about our relationships with our parents can be a useful tool in discovering a part of why we are the way we are. But — and this is a big but — parents don't play the only role in forming our inner selves. To lie on a psychoanalyst's couch for years saying "Ah-ha, now I understand why this happened!" without taking some responsibility for our behavior and what we're going to do about it is too simple, and simple ways out more often than not lead to dead ends.

When our emotional foundations are shaky, as this boy's are and mine were and yours may be, and a major crisis strikes, it enters our souls with a savage force, filling our minds with confusion and fear. We have no refuge within, no safe place.

The Three Stages

I think it's important to know what is happening to you before and during a crisis, as well as how to recover from one. You may be at any one of three stages — heading for a fall, hitting the bottom, or beginning anew — or you may be trying to help someone on the road to recovery. If you are in the first two stages yourself, you will see from my own experiences and those of others in this book that you are not alone in what you are feeling now. And if you are a helper, you will be better able to understand what your friend, relative, patient, or client is experiencing and, through that knowledge, be in a better position to help.

Heading for a Fall

Many of us whose quests for an inner home were derailed long ago by our personal myths look for easy ways out. By adopting negative beliefs about ourselves and enacting them in the way we run our lives, we often embark on a treadmill of self-deception and ultimately self-defeat. As life goes on, it becomes increasingly harder to maintain the facade. The expectations imposed upon us by ourselves and others who have been taken in by our disguises become oppressive. Not being honest with ourselves or the world is hard work, and at some point we don't want to work at it any more. Unfortunately, when it's the only way we're used to functioning and seemingly has worked in the past, we find it impossible to step off the treadmill. Instead, we turn to shortcuts and quick fixes to fill the void inside — overwork, withdrawal from others, drugs, alcohol, promiscuity, gambling — the list is a long one.

One thought we all share at this stage is "I'm losing control of my life." We go through the motions, but because we are trapped by our myths, we feel we have little control over our destinies or even our own identities. This sense of powerlessness is chilling. It sets us apart from other people, sometimes making us act in ways that serve to enhance the alienation we feel. Normally, I'm a gregarious man, yet during this period of my life, I lived in an apartment that only my children saw on a regular basis. For two and a half years, very few of my friends were ever invited to visit and then only infrequently. You may also have found ways to keep other people at arm's length.

When we add to this a lack of enthusiasm for most aspects of our lives and pride in ourselves or our actions, we feel further estranged. This is part of a process called demoralization. Demoralization refers to that empty feeling that prevents enthusiasm for anything. Life becomes perfunctory, with a sense of futility. Although not clinically depressed, demoralized individuals are dispirited. They feel they have little to believe in, whether it's personal values or ideological or spiritual concerns.

Low self-esteem is a given at this point. We simply don't like ourselves. Along with low self-esteem comes a lack of energy and motivation. There is frequent self-criticism and a view of ourselves as losers, or bad, or inferior.

At this time in our lives, we may have difficulty actually "seeing" the world around us. There seems to be a glass wall separating us from everyone and everything else. It's easy to forget there is beauty out there, and when we do notice it, the discrepancy between it and how we feel is agonizing. When I lived in California, the state had one of the highest suicide rates in North America; it still does. Part of the reason for this is the high expectations of the people who are drawn there, but another reason is the magnificent setting and the contrast it provides for people who are feeling depressed.

Alienation, demoralization, and low self-esteem are, in my experience, common feelings experienced by many people in this situation. These sad, self-flagellating feelings are often buried or walled off when we go about our day's activities but resurface during the early dawn. In fact, a hallmark of clinical depression is early morning wakefulness, accompanied by sad thoughts. This time of day is quiet, and the lack of external stimulation enables the inner torment to take center stage and become magnified beyond reality.

Like trains speeding out of control, we're going to run out of track. When we do encounter major upheavals in our lives, we run off the rails, or, to change metaphor, we hit rock bottom.

Hitting Rock Bottom

As we hit rock bottom, feelings of alienation, demoralization, and low self-esteem become unbearable. One woman I know described this time as "a tunnel of hell." Spirits broken, we can barely muster the energy to confront life's little tasks, never mind the seemingly insurmountable hurdles that loom ahead. Paradoxically, our worst fears, which our myth-driven behaviors were meant to prevent, have been realized with a vengeance. Fear of failure has turned into failure. Fear of rejection has turned into rejection. Our only choices seem to be remaining in this hopeless state or suicide.

We all differ as to what our lowest emotional point is. Throughout life, we all make mistakes and, in coping with our problems, have different levels of resourcefulness and tolerance of stress. I might lose sleep, you might turn to sleep; I might get palpitations, you might get a rash; I might exercise more, you might exercise less. For either internally driven or externally controlled reasons, we often do decide to modify our behaviors and to assume control over our lives. But for some of us, it is often too little, too late. There seems to be as much to lose by dramatically changing direction as by continuing on our destructive paths. In desperation, most of us fall back on the familiar denial behaviors we have used in the past, a kind of "I'll be okay if I work harder, or drink more, or take more drugs" attitude. This, however, serves only to aggravate the problem.

Our feelings during this time range from disbelief to anger to guilt. The profound sense of loss that many people feel during a crisis, be it the sudden collapse of a close relationship, dismissal from a job, or a serious health problem, is often met with "I can't believe this is happening to me." Despite the fact that many of us have been heading for a fall for months or even years, we feel this should be happening to someone else. This initial disbelief is often followed by anger. We look for someone to blame — specific individuals, God, society, the world. Some of us begin to blame ourselves for being the cause of our own demise, hurting others, or at least colluding with circumstances that helped perpetuate a destructive process. All of these feelings can result in an obsessional self-hatred.

There is no more lonely time than this. I remember being away on a four-day speaking engagement. It was midwinter and I flew back in a storm. By the time I got back to my apartment, I was exhausted, cold, and hungry. The simple act of entering the dark entrance hall and turning on the light was daunting. The starkness of the place, which I had made little attempt to warm in any personal way, appalled me. The first thing I noticed as I walked into the living room was that no one had left a message on my new answering machine. Just the sight of that red flashing light would have cheered me up. Its absence chilled me emotionally as much as the cold outside had chilled me physically. For months I had been dealing with my family, dealing with the hospital department I was running, dealing with a television show I appeared on — dealing, dealing, dealing — without ever dealing with myself, my pain, my guilt, or my loneliness.

Eventually we reach a crossroads. In the development of the brain and nervous system during pregnancy and shortly after birth, there is a period called the critical period. It refers to specific moments in time when the development of the brain and body can take radically different paths according to external factors such as temperature change or medication. When we are confronted with major choices that seem mutually exclusive in our adult lives, this is our critical period. It can last for a few days, weeks, or even months, but it is always temporary. It must come to an end, because if we don't change something ourselves, circumstances will force us to make a decision. It is a crucial time for any of us and can determine regression or progression, entrenchment or change, failure or success. For many, it means choosing between life and death. It is at this point that we come closest to what we are all about.

During this critical period, we arrive at a moment of truth. We look in the mirror and hate what we see and realize we can't go on. The pain brought on by our destructive activities has become worse than the pain we were trying to avoid. In the same type of flash experienced by people about to die, many of us relive our past. Then, in a startling instant, everything becomes very clear and a path opens up into the future. This sudden shake-up in our soul frees us to make new choices, choices we wouldn't have dared to consider just hours earlier. After days or weeks of misery, this single exciting moment of clarity is magical.

"Do You Believe in Magic?" was one of my favorite songs of the sixties. Many of us who were in our youth at that time did have magical expectations of the changes that were possible in individuals, and even in nations. We were sure it could be done suddenly and dramatically merely by wishing and willing it to be so. But basic, intrinsic change is a slow painful process. If it only took a moment of clarity, then many men and women caught in a web of conflict would be able to extricate themselves as soon as they "saw the light," but it just doesn't work like that.

The transition period between hitting rock bottom and a commitment to change feels enormously risky. Our personal myths must be abandoned and our poor emotional foundations razed. We feel in great danger of losing ourselves. In some ways, we think, it might be easier to put up with our present condition rather than beginning over. This questioning of our decision to change is necessary; otherwise, our commitment to turning our lives around doesn't last.

How then do you get beyond that moment of truth or even find it in the first place? First, you can't do it alone. Too many of us think that reaching out to others for help is a sign of weakness or an exercise in futility. "I don't need someone to tell me I'm depressed" is a common refrain. As a psychiatrist, I certainly could diagnose myself, but knowing that I was depressed was very different from doing something about it, and to do something about it I needed help.

In teaching mental health workers how they can assist someone in crisis, I ask them to imagine that they are putting an arm around their client's shoulders. With this action, they are saying to that person, "I am with you. I am going to help you and support you and care for you." In addition to being an arm of comfort, it is an arm of strength. It is also saying, "I am not going to allow you to do things that are self-destructive. Your abuse of your body and your mind must stop." An arm of rescue doesn't just mean unequivocal support. With support comes limit-setting, too.

We all need an arm of support at this time in our lives. Finding one can be pivotal, not only in helping us to look in the mirror but also to start us on the road to recovery. The nine people you will meet in the following chapters are not psychiatric patients. Some of them did consult me, but others sought help from various sources — family members, friends, clergy, other members of the helping professions, and self-help groups.

In addition to needing this support, though, you must want it and seek it out yourself. In my profession, I've learned over the years that I can't help people turn their lives around unless they are committed to change. Nor is anyone going to turn up on your doorstep saying, "Here I am. I'm going to change your life for you." It is entirely probable that people you know have tried to help in the past but have been turned away. Many of us play a part in arranging our own isolation. When we are verbally abusive or rejecting in other ways too many times, people stop trying. I know that when I was lonely and nobody phoned, I played a role in that. A part of me knew that there were people who cared for me — and certainly I knew where to find professional guidance! — but first I had to find the will to reach out to others.

How do you find that will? It's true that a basic level of energy is necessary in order to even make the decision to take charge of one's life. When one is depressed, it feels like an impossible task to gather the necessary psychological and physical force to initiate a resolution to change, let alone effect the change itself. Paradoxically, finding that energy is not without danger. It is when suicidal people become energized that they are in the most danger, because it is only then that they can empower themselves to commit an extraordinarily difficult act. The people in this book found the will to reject suicide and to make dramatic and difficult transformations in their lives. The energy they used to hate themselves, to hide away from other people, and to set up a sham existence was rechanneled and used to initiate action

— phoning parents or friends; asking for help from a professional; calling a self-help group; attending church or synagogue; signing up for a course; volunteering to help others.

That will also comes from a hidden core of confidence in ourselves. Few of us come through life without some successes in our past. If we search hard enough, even after a lengthy period of personal decline, we can often find a residue of that inner strength. Sometimes it is a family's history of past successes, or its spirit or strength, that provides a nucleus of confidence once it is retrieved from memory. Or sometimes it is looking back over our lives and rediscovering our successes, even as small children. What times in your life were you happy? When did you feel loved? When did you have close friends? When did you feel productive? When did you feel you could relax? Success, like failure, is self-reinforcing. Your answers to these questions can provide a small kernel of self-esteem that can be built upon.

And finally, and perhaps most importantly, the will comes from realizing that we must accept a high degree of responsibility for the life we have led. Without letting go of our anger and the blaming of others for our problems, we can't go forward.

The journey from crisis to rebirth is filled with self-doubt and the cynicism or hostility of those we have hurt, but from within and from the people we enlist to guide us we can find the will to begin again.

New Beginnings

Our turnarounds consist of a number of important ingredients: a confrontation with ourselves and a recognition of our personal responsibility in our downfalls; a crystallization of our conflicted thoughts and feelings; a decision to give up our dishonesty with ourselves and others; and a motivation to change.

There is a point after we have made the decision to change where we all have to ask ourselves, "If I am going to have some sort of new life, how do I avoid having the exact same life I had before?" In my own case, I found a therapist and started reaching out to my family and friends. I made an effort to rediscover my spiritual roots, and I started thinking about not only what I had been doing that was self-destructive but also what I had been doing that was unrewarding. It was time to work on my emotional foundations and to ask myself those timeless questions that most of us have avoided over the years — Who am I and who do I want to be? Are my relationships meaningful and honest? Why am I here? Is it God, caring for others, for a creative purpose? What do I really want to do with my life and how do I go about achieving those goals?

If we can restructure our lives so that those three building blocks of self-esteem, belonging, and believing are areas that we consciously work on alone and with others, rather than expecting them to be handed to us on a silver platter, our lives will open up and become enriched. This rebuilding process is made up of small steps, each one leading to a measure of freedom and joy that has been missing in our lives. One of these is rediscovering old pastimes that we had left behind. These may be very simple pleasures. For example, a woman I know, whose marriage had ended suddenly, found the courage to eat in a restaurant by herself. Although she is a great lover of food, she had found it impossible to eat out on her own after her husband left. That simple act of going to a restaurant helped lift her spirits.

Another step is looking realistically at who we are and who we would like to be. How large is the gap separating the two? It's common for insecure people to have lofty goals they know they can never reach, thereby condemning themselves to a life of unfulfillment. Setting up more realistic targets, which are more congruent with who you really are rather than who you used to think you should be, is more rewarding and a great deal less stressful.

Abandoning our old personal myths and accepting ourselves as flawed but worthwhile human beings in turn enhances our relationships with others. I used to think the advice to "love yourself first" was a rather stupid cliché, but I now believe that, like all clichés, it holds a simple truth. If you care about yourself and care for others, they will care for you. Caring for yourself doesn't mean self-aggrandizement, it means appreciating yourself and accepting that you have strengths and weaknesses like everyone else. And caring for others means lifting your eyes from your own navel long enough to appreciate other people for who they really are, too, rather than who you think they should be. Helping others —friends, strangers, fellow members of a support group — can also be a way to bolster our own self-esteem and sense of belonging.

Developing a belief or values system is a journey in itself. Some of the people in this book rediscover their childhood faiths, others investigate different religions than the one they were raised in, or they consult psychics or astrologers. Other people I have known became involved in a cause they believe in — saving the environment, world peace, caring for disadvantaged children. And still others make pilgrimages to sacred places, attend spiritual retreats, or simply read books examining philosophical topics. The means is unimportant. What is important is the spiritual comfort provided by rediscovering or discovering a belief or values system.

I found that my patients were a constant source of inspiration for me during this time. I marveled at their courage, at what they could accomplish when every strike seemed to be against them. One person in particular comes to mind. Donny attempted suicide at age sixteen and, after being admitted to hospital, was diagnosed as having schizophrenia. After a year in hospital, he was sent to a group home where I first met him. He had grown up in a poverty-stricken immigrant family laden with problems. His father was a violent alcoholic, his mother was chronically depressed, his unemployed older brother was abusive, his younger brother was autistic, and his sister was a drug addict and prostitute. At the group home, Donny met adults who, for the first time in his life, believed in him and in turn he began to believe in himself. Although he received no emotional or financial support from his family after he left the group home, he pushed himself through his remaining years at high school and was accepted into a university remedial program for people with learning disabilities. On weekends and holidays, he worked with handicapped children and at part-time jobs. He was able to complete two half years of credits before he was forced to quit to help out in his father's small garage. Although his family life remains unsettled — his father and mother are separating and his sister is pregnant — he so firmly believes in his own worth that he has been able to rise above his negative home environment to claim a better life for himself. Right now, he has a lead on a job as a program organizer for inner-city children. I can't think of a better way for him to put his new enthusiasm for life to work.

Donny and all the men and women in this book reached deep into their souls and decided to turn their lives around. Their choice was to live or die, and they chose to live. No matter what you have lost, it is important to remember that there is a way back and there are people who can help you find that way.

The Role of Helper

If you have bought this book because you want to help someone you know who is in crisis, you may be feeling at a loss yourself. To help someone close to us who is in great distress often feels like an enormous responsibility. Many people wonder if they are even qualified to help. The truth of the matter is that any caring individual can serve as a crucial helper to someone in trouble.

When I tell people this, they often respond with "But I don't know what to do or say." If we are respectful, honest, and available in our relationships with a troubled man, woman, or adolescent, we are doing our part. Although we may not think that our actions or words are having any positive effect at all, we must remember that the person in need must be ready to accept help. At some time, our compassionate — or even irreverent, teasing, or confrontative — messages may hit home, but only when our friend or relative is open to understanding and acting on our words. That part is entirely up to them.

Sometimes a helper can become so involved in a close friend or relative's problems that they become emotionally overburdened. One of my patients is married to a man who was fired from a high-paying job and is about to be arrested for income tax evasion. Her closest friend just gave birth to a child with major birth defects. Since these two events, she has overextended herself helping these two people close to her and has been unable to stop crying. She realized that she needed help coping with these two crises and came to me. It's important to recognize the ripple effect a crisis can have and to seek out help before you, too, are sucked into the whirlpool of someone else's pain. There is a truism in twelve-step recovery programs to the effect that nobody can do it alone. We all need a helping hand of some sort when we are in deep trouble and, by the same token, we can offer our hand to those who are in need. At times, of course, the hand (and arm) belongs to a designated professional helper, but not in the majority of instances. In the ensuing examples you will see an array of people who were "there" for friends and acquaintances, and made a vital difference.

Part One
The Young Quest

I once met at a reception a thirteen-year-old girl who exuded what is popularly called "personality." Her self-assurance and warmth drew people of all ages to her, and although she was so young, you could see that she was at peace with herself and those around her. What has taken me half a century to achieve, she had gained at age thirteen. For most of us, though, it takes much longer.

Finding our inner homes is rarely resolved in adolescence. It is a quest that begins there. In classifying the tasks involved in that adolescent search for identity, I've always found it interesting that they all start with the letter I. They consist of impulse control (sexual and aggressive), independence, individuation, intimacy, industry, initiative, and ideology. How successfully we complete each of these tasks helps decide what kinds of independent beings we are going to be. Until this stage in our lives, we are under the wing of our parents, authority figures who tell us what to do, nurture us, and confront us when we stray. As we grow older, we must serve as our own guides and consciences. The process of adolescence is weaning ourselves away from our parents and adopting some of the parental roles for ourselves.

The hallmark of this process, as opposed to almost any other time of life other than the first few months, is the rapidity of change. We change physically, hormonally, emotionally, and cognitively. We act differently and reason differently. Our physical changes preoccupy us. Teen-agers are constantly comparing their newly developed sexual characteristics, as well as their skin, weight, and height, with their peers. Whether our new appearance is attractive to the opposite sex if we are heterosexual or to the same sex if we are homosexual is an issue of major concern. Hundreds of years ago, the concerns of adolescents were the same as they are now. Basically, they can be expressed in a single question: Am I acceptable or am I going to be rejected?

We use our family, friends, and other people to answer that question and to enable us to see what our image is really like. If that image is distorted, life becomes an uphill battle of living a lie. We keep perpetuating our negative myths until they get us into serious enough trouble that we are forced to confront ourselves.

At a group home for adolescents, I've been working with an eighteen-year-old girl who was kicked out of her upper-middle-class home three months ago. Since the age of three, Sara had been called an "evil little girl" by her grandmother, who lived with the family. At the age of eleven, she found out that she had been adopted. That news coupled with the constant derision from her grandmother set her off on a self-destructive path. Her rebellious behavior increased to the point that the family was unable to cope with her. Today, you wouldn't recognize the new Sara if you had known the old one. She has so abruptly turned herself around that one wonders if it isn't an act, but it isn't. In a group meeting, she told the other teen-agers at the home, "I realize now that what my grandmother told me was wrong. I'm not a bad person. I'm a good person." The acting she was doing was then, not now. She had been living up to a message that wasn't valid.

When crisis strikes an adolescent who is undergoing not only the instability that characterizes this period, but also the erosion of their emotional foundations from without and within, it can prove to be particularly debilitating. Teen-

agers are considered to be narcissistic. They are preoccupied with the "I." The paradox of narcissism is that, as
adolescents, we think we are unique. When we are in trouble, we believe we are the only ones going through this hell
of loneliness, low self-esteem, pain, and fear. "What should I
do?" and "Whom should I confide in?" are questions we have
a great deal of difficulty answering. We want to do the one
"right thing" that will gain acceptance from friends, parents, and especially ourselves, but we are so afraid of being
ostracized or laughed at or not taken seriously that we
remain isolated rather than confiding our difficulties to
others. This is particularly true of adolescent boys, many of
whom believe that letting other people know about their
vulnerabilities is a sign of weakness.

Adults, in turn, may not be sensitive to a young person's
suffering. Anna Freud's concept of Sturm und Drang
(storminess and turbulence) as an almost inevitable charac-
teristic of adolescence has colored our thinking. Although
most teen-agers pass through this stage of life fairly
smoothly, many adults believe that this period is always
marked by upheaval. For this reason, when a young person
close to them does get into trouble, they often dismiss the
warning signs as part and parcel of a stage that will be
outgrown. In fact, adolescents in significant trouble will not
grow out of their problems without help. In many cases,
they do want to confide in their parents or another adult, but
one of the most common complaints of adolescents is that
adults are uninterested, or unavailable, or unable to talk to
them. "They wouldn't understand" is perhaps the most
frequently heard comment.

When adolescents are unable to resolve their problems on
their own, they seek the same escapes from a painful reality
as adults. Alcohol and other drugs lead the way in providing
temporary relief. This shouldn't surprise us: young people

are simply following our adult example. In our culture, the use of drugs, from liquor to tranquilizers, is widely recognized and often accepted. Although many adults believe there is an epidemic of drug use among teen-agers, in reality the use of drugs by high-school students seems to have plateaued over the past few years. It's true that many young people experiment with drugs, but only a small minority get into real trouble. That said, physical evidence of a teen-ager's drug abuse includes dilated pupils or needle marks, reddened nostrils, or, obviously, the discovery of pills, syringes, or other drug paraphernalia in the child's room. The signs of deep emotional distress, however, are more significant. They may exist whether the child is using drugs or not. They include difficulties in sleeping or changes in sleeping patterns; poor personal hygiene; a decline in school performance; rapid mood changes or an increasing tendency to be moody or withdrawn; difficulty in concentrating; and a change in relationships with friends or family. It is important to know that while a child can be helped with his or her substance abuse, it is necessary, and in some ways more important, to address the underlying emotional problems.

One factor that compounds these problems is the unpredictability of change in our rapidly changing world. It used to be that a young person would learn a skill, join a company after graduation, and stay with that company until he retired. Today, in many fields, we can only guess at what skills will be needed in the future. Parents are no longer able to advise their children with any certainty about what courses they should take to secure a job. The rising divorce rate also contributes to the uncertainty of life for many teen-agers. They can no longer count on the structure of their families remaining the same throughout their adolescence. It's little wonder that when they do encounter major difficulties, they sometimes feel very alone in a pressure-filled, unstable world.

When adolescents in crisis hit rock bottom, they consider suicide as a way to escape from their problems. In this they resemble all age groups. Very few people go through life without thinking at one time or other about killing themselves; however, most people, including teen-agers, don't have a well-thought-out plan. Although the media would have us believe that there is an "epidemic" of teen-age suicide, the suicide rate for this age group plateaued over the past few years; the rate is much higher in the elderly and middle-aged. It is the tragedy of premature death that attracts media attention and unfortunately may contribute to "copycat" suicides of other impressionable youths. Nevertheless, failed suicide attempts or threats should always be taken seriously. A person who is so bereft of other resources that he or she has to resort to these measures to attract attention is someone with very serious problems. They are also at risk because an attempt can easily slip into the real thing. How then do we help adolescents before they reach this stage?

First and foremost, they need to know they are loved. The capacity to give and receive love is absolutely essential for healthy emotional growth. Children are never too old to be told in words and by actions that they are special. When parents reach out to their children and create a climate of empathy and understanding in the home, their adolescents will tend to feel more comfortable talking to them about their problems.

On the other hand, teen-agers also need space and time to learn about themselves and to make mistakes. There are times when it is appropriate to let the young people we care about know that we have certain expectations of them and times when it is appropriate to stand back and give them the space they need. Neither may seem like expressions of love, but they are two of the more important ones I know. Another one is setting limits. Living by certain rules or standards of behavior is a part of the learning process of childhood and adolescence. Raising our children to be responsible individuals is another sign that we care. Our love coupled with limit-setting provides that helping arm of comfort and strength that we all need from time to time, but perhaps most crucially during adolescence.

In addition to their parents' love and acceptance, peers are also important in developing a teen-ager's self-esteem and sense of belonging. This is why self-help groups of teen-agers who suffer from the same problems can be an effective way to help a child in crisis. And, finally, other adults who serve as models or mentors — teachers, mental health professionals, coaches, family friends, or relatives — can play an important role in leading a troubled young person in exciting new directions. Outer-directed, meaningful activities, such as volunteer work, are particularly helpful in this regard.

Like all of us, adolescents need to believe in something. Our secular, materialistic society hasn't served our children well in this area. I'm not suggesting that we march our kids off to church or synagogue, particularly if religion doesn't play a part in our own lives. Parents who drop their children off at a place of worship while they go off to brunch are not doing their sons and daughters any favors. Children learn by modeling themselves after adults. If parents contribute to those who are less fortunate through volunteering, or if they work for an environmental or political cause, or if they have religious convictions they are willing to share rather than foist upon their children, their youngsters will have the opportunity to become involved in meaningful activities that will help them develop a belief system of their own.

The crises of the three adolescents whose stories are told in the following pages are precipitated by a number of different factors. There are many others that can also way-lay people of this age in their quest for an inner home; however, regardless of the type of problem, the result of each is an onslaught on a teen-ager's self-esteem, sense of belonging, and belief system. That Timothy, Anna, and Linda were able to turn their lives around at a time of life marked by rapid change and uncertainty should provide hope for all of us.

2. Different and Not Proud of It

HIS MOTHER STOOD WITH HIM AT THE BEGINNING of a long hallway. After nervously checking her watch, she sent him off toward the closed door at the hall's end as if the small blond boy were embarking on a perilous journey. She patted him on the shoulder, murmured a few encouraging words, gave him a gentle push. Timothy hugged the fourth-grade report card with its checklist of Cs and Ds and walked slowly to the study door. He turned around to look at his mother, she nodded her head, and he knocked. Inside, a man's voice impatiently gave him permission to enter.

Behind a massive desk, Jean Deauville — well-known political scientist and Timothy's father — presided over tidy piles of reports with a Scotch in one hand and a Dictaphone in the other. The curtains were drawn although it was a beautiful late spring day. A nearly empty crystal decanter perched on a stack of books. Jean Deauville didn't welcome his only child but snatched the report card from the boy's hand, first scanning the marks and then beginning to read the teacher's report. Timothy stared down at the Oriental carpet. He pretended his shoe was a car traveling along one of the soft curved lines, racing away.

His foot had reached the corner of the desk when his father rose. There was no sound when the blow came. Without a word, his father struck him with the heel of his hand, knocking Timothy to the floor. Jean Deauville then stepped over his son and strode unsteadily out of the room to find his wife.

When Tim told me this story from his childhood, he was a young man. The story was told as young men often tell such stories, with a mixture of embarrassment and pain. He admitted that although this was the first time his father had struck him, it was not the first episode of violence in the family. He had seen his father berate and slap his mother on several occasions, always after bouts of drinking. And while these attacks on his mother didn't hurt him physically, they left him with a sick feeling inside and a sense of powerlessness and rage — "One of my earliest memories is kneeling with my mother at the foot of her bed after one of my father's tirades. She was crying. I was crying. The lights were out and the room seemed enormous, like it was swallowing us up."

Tim's inner home as a boy was filled with those emotions that leave us spiritual orphans — fear, self-loathing, and loneliness. As the only child in a wealthy home, he spent more time with a succession of immigrant housekeepers than he did with his own parents. His father was often traveling, and his mother, when she was not teaching high-school French, was taking courses at university. When the family came together, their roles were rigidly set. Tim's petite, dark-haired mother, Suzanne, was required to provide an environment in which her important husband could think and write. She did this by constantly shushing their son — "I think I learned to say shhhh before I learned to talk" — all the while reminding him of his duty to respect and honor his tall, physically imposing father. Tim's role was to act the proper upper-class scion — intelligent, popular, sports-minded. That he was none of these was anathema to his father.

"My father was always starting sentences with 'No son of mine. . . .' I suppose this sounds kind of stupid, but I used to call myself Noson. I used to fantasize about being called Myson." It was not to be. As bright as Timothy was and as hard as he tried, he could do no better at school because of a learning disability that wasn't identified until Grade Five. He was behind in reading, he reversed letters, and his script was illegible and full of spelling errors. The "diagnosis" did nothing to placate Jean Deauville. He firmly believed his son's inability to succeed at school was due to a lack of motivation and drive and a mother who was too indulgent.

As the years went by, remedial reading classes, special tutoring, and Tim's own ability to compensate for his disability enabled him to pass each school year, but he was never able to even approach the academic excellence expected of him by his father. In fact, he found that although he was able to understand the material in high school, when he sat down to write an exam, what he thought he knew seemed to dissolve from his mind. He "choked" whenever his performance was on the line.

This tremendous fear of failure steered Tim away from playing competitive sports, particularly the ones that his father held dear. Instead, the lanky teen-ager enjoyed spending hours running or bicycling through the quiet ravines that wound their way through his neighborhood. The exhilarating feeling of speed and being in touch with his body drove away his father's disdainful image of him that was by now firmly rooted in his own consciousness. For a short time, the shy failure became the star racer.

Tim's ability to pretend, to erect walls around the inner pain caused by his personal myth that he would never be good enough, increased as he entered his middle teens. He attended a local high school where the children of the intellectual elite of the city were routinely sent. It was in this school that Tim realized that famous and powerful fathers could also be warm and caring parents. He began to pretend that he too had one of these model fathers. He pretended that his scholastic failures didn't plague him. He pretended that nothing was wrong. But at sixteen, the walls Tim had unconsciously built to protect himself began to fail him.

Heading for a Fall

With children his own age, Tim was always somewhat shy. Being timid is not unusual for only children who are frequently left to their own devices. However, Tim's shyness stemmed from feeling different from other boys his age and not knowing why — "In high school, in the locker room after gym class, I just didn't feel like smacking other guys with towels or telling dirty jokes or anything like that. And when I did try, just to be like everybody else, it never felt right." The sexual experiences, real or imagined, of other boys held no interest for him. Explicit photos in the magazines that his friends hid under their mattresses turned him off rather than on.

The reasons for these reactions remained unclear to Tim until shortly before his sixteenth birthday. It was then that he developed what could only be described as a crush on one of his male classmates. His feelings for that young lad were a forerunner to similar romantic yearnings for other boys in the months that followed, accompanied by masturbatory fantasies that were decidedly homosexual in nature. These new feelings filled him with terror. He found it difficult to meet the eyes of his classmates, thinking that they would somehow know. He skipped gym class as often as he could. He once found the courage to furtively buy gay magazines at a downtown variety store and then worried all the way home that he would meet someone he knew and be found out. He was even more terrified that the magazines would be found by his parents, so he hid them in the attic.

At an age when it was important to be like everyone else, Tim felt that he was the only one who was completely different — in his relationship with his father, in his schoolwork, and now in his sexual orientation. Unlike other gay teen-agers who try to deny their homosexuality by dating girls, Tim decided to avoid the issue altogether. He built another image — that of the shy boy who doesn't date — and hid behind it. For a while this seemed to work. He became adept at pretending to be shy around girls. "It was quite easy actually, because I never was an outgoing sort of person."

Such walls, though, need only one little crack to send them tumbling down. In Tim's case, it was his only friends, Jon and Andrew, who discovered his secret. True to the self-deprecation that marked his feelings about himself, Tim could never understand why these two academically bright boys bothered with him. It never occurred to him that he had qualities that matched theirs — intelligence, quiet humor, and a lack of macho affectation. Instead, he considered himself lucky to have two friends whom he trusted.

The trust ended on a morning hike in the fall. "It was one of those mornings when you feel really good to be alive. My father had been overseas for a few weeks, and there I was walking through this incredibly beautiful valley with two good friends. I wasn't even thinking about being gay or

anything and then it started." Jon and Andrew began ex-
changing crude jokes, making fun of gays, not an unusual
pastime for seventeen-year-olds. Tim, though, had never
heard them do it before. He had learned to ignore such jokes
when other classmates told them, but hearing them told by
his two closest friends touched a very sensitive chord. The
reason for his silence and unease was not difficult to guess.

Jon and Andrew weren't insensitive dolts given to crude
humor at other people's expense. Sometimes even the most
tolerant and progressive men and women lapse into preju-
diced humor in private, poking fun at every imaginable
group. The boys fell silent and then apologized to Tim.
"They told me that they had no idea and I believed them, but
I just couldn't handle it. I took off."

Over the next few days, both friends left messages for
Tim, which he didn't return. Monday came and he skipped
school. He pretended he was sick with the flu the entire
week. To his mother's anxious queries, he responded with
offhand comments about not feeling well or being worried
about exams. He couldn't tell his mother; he felt she had
enough to worry about without having his homosexuality to
deal with, too. On the Sunday, to avoid his mother calling the
family doctor, he told her that he was feeling better and was
going to school the next day.

That night Tim lay awake in bed, willing the darkness to
remain so that he wouldn't have to face his classmates. He
imagined the whispers about his homosexuality being
passed from one person to the next, their eyes widening in
surprise, or mock horror, or actual disgust. Despite the fact
that he had heard that being homosexual was no longer
considered psychiatrically abnormal, the slurs of the ill-
informed darted around in his head all night long.

The next morning Tim was exhausted. He badly needed
some words of encouragement and love, but his mother had

already left the house to attend an early staff meeting. At his locker, Jon and Andrew approached him separately. "Both of them said they still wanted to be friends. It was the word 'still' that got to me. I made each of them promise not to tell anybody, not that it did any good. I figured everybody knew."

With all of his flimsy walls destroyed, Tim felt incredibly naked and alone. The most intimate fact of his short life was public knowledge. Feeling betrayed by his own mind, body, and friends, he imagined classmates were looking at him, talking behind his back, laughing, perhaps even planning to hurt him.

Adding to his anguish was a growing fear that he would fail his final exams and be ineligible for college. The past year had seen his academic performance slip even further, earning disparaging rebukes from his father. For Tim, seventeen and standing as tall as Jean Deauville, the abuse was no longer physical. His father's tongue, though, continued to be as effective as his hand had been in smashing his son's ego. Imagining his father's reaction to the news that his heir was a homosexual filled Tim with sick apprehension.

Tim desperately needed to talk to someone. He had an uncle on the west coast, whom he had met once and liked tremendously. His father's older brother was everything Jean Deauville was not — warm, humorous, and low-key. However, Tim couldn't imagine picking up the phone and blurting out that he was gay to a man he'd met only once. He had rebuffed Jon and Andrew's attempts to be friendly, so they were out of the question. The guidance counselor at school was also struck off the list because Tim couldn't risk the news of his homosexuality getting back to his parents. Going to confession was another option, but he hadn't gone to church for years and had doubts about a priest being able to help. Finally, he considered contacting the Homosexual

Counseling Center listed in the telephone directory only to decide that the people there had a vested interest in his pursuing a life as a gay man. Being gay had brought Tim nothing but pain. The last thing he wanted to do was follow a homosexual life style. "I had read about homosexuality but I still thought that maybe it was some strange obsession that could be cured. I didn't know where to go to find out."

Alone in his room, night after night, Tim searched for a way out. His schoolbooks were rarely opened. It was on one such evening that he overheard his parents arguing. It was late and Jean Deauville had had too much to drink, yet again. Tim's mother was pleading with her husband to talk to their son, who was obviously in need of help. The more she pleaded, the angrier he became. He saw no reason to discuss anything with Tim; Tim was her responsibility; as his mother, she had ruined him. At the sound of shattering glass, Tim reexperienced the rising sense of panic that engulfed him whenever his parents' arguments became violent. As a small boy, he had hidden under his bed. Now he stood at the top of the stairs, hating his own passivity and his father's aggression. "I just turned to stone. But when I heard Mom yell, 'Don't hit me,' something snapped and I ran downstairs and into the room where they were. I think they were both surprised to see me. Everything kind of stopped. Nobody said a thing. And then we all just went to bed."

The next morning, a school day, Tim slept in. His father was waiting for him when he came downstairs for breakfast. For a moment, Tim thought the man wanted to apologize for the previous evening, but those hopes faded as soon as he sat down at the table. Instead of an apology, Jean Deauville looked up from the morning paper and launched into a lecture on being late for school. The lecture rapidly turned into a personal attack, covering all the old flaws that he wanted his son and wife to correct. Throughout the speech, Suzanne Deauville sat with head bent and eyes fixed on her cup of coffee. She didn't say a word.

Tim's dash into the room to protect his mother the night before perhaps subconsciously gave him the courage to do what he did next. At the end of Jean Deauville's diatribe, as he prepared to leave the room for work, Tim suddenly rose from the table, grabbed his father by the tie, and pushed him up against a wall. All the hurt and anger that he had stored inside for years shook in his voice as he warned his father never to lay a hand on his mother again. "I told him I'd kill him if he ever did it again. And then I just let go and ran out of the room. Later on, I felt good about shutting up the great man, but at the time I felt really sick about it. I felt out of control, no better than him."

Standing up to his father provided a release of sorts for Tim; however, it didn't solve his problems. After the confrontation in the breakfast room, his father was rarely home, and his mother seemed to be going through her own crisis. Her haggard appearance alarmed Tim, making him feel responsible for the failure of his parents' marriage and further strengthening his resolve not to involve his mother in his own troubles. He lost what interest he had had in school, slept in most mornings, and stayed up late at night smoking grass and listening to music or watching talk shows. The joints he had begun to smoke several times a day were the only things he looked forward to and were possibly the only remaining reason for going to school. They weren't enough. Tim didn't make it to the end of his senior year.

Hitting Rock Bottom

Bereft of any meaningful support from his family and suffering from the loss of his two closest friends, Tim was truly isolated. He was slipping gradually but unmistakably into a deep depression and began to actively contemplate suicide. Jumping off a nearby bridge into the ravine had been a recurring fantasy. He imagined each step — getting high on dope, approaching the bridge, placing his hands on the rail, floating into oblivion. As he got more depressed, he became convinced that suicide was the only way out. His daydream turned into a concrete plan, and with that plan came a curious serenity. He didn't need to worry any more about his sexuality, his ineptitude at school, or disappointing his parents.

On the night he had chosen to die, Tim sat with his mother in the sunroom overlooking the garden. "I told her I was sorry for all the trouble I'd caused her. She said the problems in the family weren't my fault, that she loved me and worried about me. You know it was probably the first time I'd ever really talked to her? I finally told her I was gay. I just blurted it out. She didn't seem surprised, said that she'd suspected for quite a while but that she'd been waiting for me to tell her. She's really terrific, you know. I guess I felt like I was saying good-bye to the one person who meant something to me."

The warm feelings toward his mother had given Tim second thoughts about killing himself, but not enough to abandon his resolve. His mother went to bed early as she did every night. Tim waited until he thought she was asleep and climbed the stairs to his room. After writing his mother a farewell note, he carefully placed it on the bed with some wild flowers he had picked earlier in the day. He tucked three joints in a pocket to smoke in the park beside the bridge, picked up a package from the desk, and slipped down the back stairs.

Suzanne Deauville was not, in fact, asleep. She had heard Tim go downstairs but not outside. For an hour afterwards, she lay awake worrying about her son until, finally, she threw on her robe and hurried down the stairs to talk to him. When she wasn't able to find him, she assumed that he had returned to his room without her hearing him. The note was the first thing she saw as she opened the door to his bedroom.

Tim had one stop to make before walking to the park. His talk with his mother had affected him more than he thought possible, and by the time he reached Andrew's house, his eyes had the bleary look of someone who has been crying. Andrew's mother answered the door and was appalled at the change in the young man who stood on her doorstep. "I must have looked like a complete wreck. I don't think I'd washed my hair in a week. I had the shakes, plus it was pretty late to be calling on a friend I hadn't seen in weeks. She must have guessed something was up."

Tim walked into Andrew's room and collapsed in a chair. Andrew was as alarmed as his mother had been at his friend's appearance and at the reason for the visit. After a largely incoherent story, Tim handed the other boy his entire collection of tapes. Andrew stared at the package dumbfounded and then realized what his friend was planning to do. "All of a sudden he got really mad. Told me that if I didn't give a shit about myself, he wasn't going to give a shit about me. I suddenly realized that to get that steamed, the guy had to care. That just blew me away. Then he lay on the guilt — talked about my mom, how there were lots of guys who were worse off than me. And I started feeling incredibly self-centered, like maybe he was right?"

Meanwhile Suzanne had phoned Andrew's mother. Panic-stricken after reading the suicide note, she had called 911. The police had arrived at the house within minutes of her call and had left with a description and a photograph of Tim. She had phoned Jean overseas, couldn't locate him, and then began to telephone Tim's friends. The call to Andrew's home was the second one she made.

By the time Suzanne arrived at the Corsons, both she and Tim were emotionally and physically drained. Andrew's mother drove them to the Emergency Room of the local hospital, where Tim was admitted to the Adolescent Psychiatric Ward. The words "psychiatric ward" carry connotations that are scary for many people. The public's contact with this part of a hospital is usually through the fictional hospitals of television and film, which are peopled with white-uniformed staff and patients wearing hospital gowns. In fact, such wards can range from high-tech-looking places to homelike settings. Staff dress informally and patients usually wear their street clothes.

On Tim's admission, Suzanne was interviewed by a social worker while Tim was taken to the ward, where he was assigned a psychiatrist and a primary care worker. A team approach is often used in treating mental health problems in a hospital setting. A psychiatrist sees the patient at a set time each day and at other times when necessary, and a primary care worker — a nurse or social worker —is assigned to look after the needs of the patient on an hour-to-hour basis. Other staff members are familiar with each case through regularly held meetings.

For the first few days after his admission to the hospital, Tim was not allowed to contact or visit with his family or they with him. This is usual in such cases. Because family problems are often a contributing factor in suicide attempts, it is felt that a brief separation between the patient and his parents is necessary until he is stabilized. The social worker assigned to the family kept the Deauvilles informed of his progress.

That first night in hospital, as Tim lay in bed, he was surprised to discover that for some strange reason he was not upset at his failure to end his life. For the first time he was relieved that he had failed at something. His talks with his mother and Andrew had forced him to think about himself and his life. Why should he expect everyone to feel sorry for him? Were his problems that insurmountable? Did his mother deserve this? Why was he throwing his life away? They had also forced him to admit that there were people in the world who cared for him, warts and all.

Within a few days, however, the suicidal thoughts returned, unbidden and unwelcome. Unlike the last time, he was frightened and asked his primary care worker, a nurse, for help. Tim was placed in a closely watched locked area called Constant Care, and the entire staff was alerted. After a few days he was offered, and readily agreed to, ward privileges on the condition that he would participate in the program and not make any self-destructive attempts. Back with the other teen-age patients, he participated, at first reluctantly, in group meetings and recreational activities. Although he was a loner by nature, listening to other kids talk about their problems encouraged Tim to speak about his own feelings.

Group therapy is often wrongly considered a lesser form of treatment. In fact, it can be extremely effective for all kinds of problems and for people of all ages. For adolescents, revealing oneself in a group entails exposure and the danger of humiliation in front of others. The fear of embarrassment, rejection, and even derision looms larger than life. Tim was finally able to tell his own story and express some of his fears after watching others take the risk of revealing themselves within the group, seemingly with no ill effects and with the encouragement of the group leader (in this case a nurse). He was pleased and relieved by the feedback and understanding he received from the group.

Several times in the next two weeks he would let it slip that he wanted to die and would be placed back in Constant Care. He would agree to ward privileges, thinking that he had licked his suicidal thoughts, but once in an open environment, even in the hospital, he grew frightened and arranged to have himself placed in the safety of a closed area.

New Beginnings

At a staff meeting, a young chaplaincy student, Rob Britnell, asked if he could work with Tim. In the few brief conversations that he had had with him, Rob was intrigued by Tim's mention of a major "sin" that he couldn't divulge. Rob thought that he might be able to get Tim to open up to him about his problems. As a chaplaincy student, Rob was particularly interested in Tim's concerns about sin. He also felt that he might be able to establish a special rapport with Tim if they worked together one on one. The ward chief agreed to his plan, and the next day Rob met with Tim in the cafeteria.

Tim had kept his homosexuality a secret from the staff, partly because the older male doctors reminded him of his father and partly because it was not something he felt comfortable talking about with the female mental health professionals. Against her better judgment, his mother had agreed to keep quiet about it. In contrast to the other staff, the gentle humor and warm personality of the chaplaincy student put Tim at ease. Learning that Rob had had a tough time with his own father also helped build a rapport between the two young men. Rob spent an early meeting talking about his own childhood and his dream to help inner-city teen-agers. He talked in a matter-of-fact way about helping others as a way of growing and contributing to one's sense of worth. Because there was nothing overly enthusiastic or goody-goody in the way he spoke about reaching out to other people, Tim found himself drawn to Rob's philosophy of living and to Rob personally.

They began to meet regularly, and in fact both young men were enthusiastic about the discussions. Although Rob was not gay himself, he knew many people who were. His tolerance and empathy enabled Tim to open up about his own feelings, and he found acceptance and encouragement for the first time. "Rob made me realize that I was holding back my entire life just because I was gay. I wasn't making any plans, other than killing myself, which I'd begun to realize wasn't such a great thing to look forward to." Their conversations continued for the next few weeks. Rob proved crucial in getting Tim to accept his homosexuality. Rob was not a specialist in this area; rather, he was a truly caring human being. Tim's doctor, social worker, and the other patients in his group were also deeply involved in Tim's recovery, especially after he was able to reveal his homosexuality to them.

Tim's Catholic upbringing meant that he had unusual difficulty with revealing his homosexuality. Anyone with a Catholic or fundamentalist background has the additional challenge of overcoming a belief that he or she is a sinner because of their homosexuality — in addition to the threat of being looked upon as a social pariah. Many cannot face the shame and humiliation. Not only did Tim have to face the likelihood of opprobrium and derision by many in society, but he somehow had to forget that he was designated a sinner by many in his religion.

At the end of the month, Tim was no longer feeling suicidal or as withdrawn and depressed. After a few successful day passes and some uneventful weekends at home, he was ready to leave the hospital after a six-week stay. He left with mixed emotions. The hospital felt safe. He had grown accustomed to its routines, the familiar faces of the staff, the protective blanket that institutions can wrap around their patients. Worried that he would again become suicidal after returning home, he talked to his hospital psychiatrist, who in turn referred him to me for counseling twice a week.

By the time I saw Tim he was well on his way to recovery. Rob Britnell had arranged work for him in an inner-city church-run day-care center and he planned to take correspondence courses to complete high school. During that time, working with children was especially helpful for Tim. Teen-agers who lead very private lives, as Tim had done, often blossom given the opportunity to show affection to other people. In playing with and teaching children, Tim discovered a part of himself that he didn't even know existed. Giving affection and receiving it back from preschoolers was a revelation to him. He could make people happy, he was good at it, and it was a lot more fun than staring at his own navel for days on end.

Five Years Later

Five years later, Tim is a junior at a liberal arts college. Its tolerance of individual life styles, encouragement of personal autonomy, and dedication to community work and social commitment make it an ideal school for him. The special educational coaching he receives for his learning disability is a further plus. For the first time in his life, Tim is a successful student, earning Bs and even the odd A. He lives off campus with his lover, a Chinese music student. In his spare time, he works with children in a day-care center in the area.

Tim's parents are divorced. Although he keeps in close touch with his mother, he has only recently responded to his father's attempts to get in touch with him. The experience of Tim's hospitalization and the subsequent divorce from Suzanne shook the foundations of Jean Deauville's sense of his world. He began to examine his own role in the shattering of the family. Tim could not at first bring himself to see his father because he simplistically blamed him for all his problems. Even more importantly, Tim had not yet reached the stage of accepting himself completely. It is only recently that Tim has found the inner confidence to approach his father and try to create a new relationship. He wants to discover if there is anything salvageable between them.

3. Leaving Home to Find Home

LINDA FASZLO LEFT HER FAMILY HOME AT THE age of nineteen, not a particularly unusual age for moving out. What was unusual about her leaving was that it was tense, angry, and painful. Rather than a warm good-bye between daughter and parents, Linda left with bitter accusations on both sides.

Linda was the eldest of three children in an upwardly mobile Hungarian Jewish family. Her father, Ernest, had escaped from Hungary during the Russian invasion in the late fifties. He was justifiably proud of the fact that he had left the old country with nothing and was now a successful manufacturer. Her mother, Sonja, was the antithesis of her short, plump, often crude husband. A refined woman, whose dark, striking features had been inherited by her oldest daughter, she had married Ernest at the urging of her parents. The marriage was not a happy one, and Linda and her sister, Mara, and brother, Philip, grew up in an atmosphere of silent tension.

Linda broke that silence when she began high school. In the early eighties, she was a throwback to the sixties, a sensitive, self-styled flower child immersed in a decade that she had barely known. She knew at some level that she wasn't a mystical type of person, but it became important to prove to herself and others that she believed this about herself. Actually, she didn't feel especially good about herself at all. At her large urban school, she felt most comfortable with the crowd who wore their long hair and second-hand clothing as badges identifying their artistic or political bent. Anti-establishment, anti-nuclear war, pro-environment, she ventured in her young opinions as far left as possible from her father's capitalist world view. "I started challenging what he was saying at the dinner table. He was such a middle-class chauvinist, a little Napoleon. I felt a certain power in being able to start him off on a tirade, although I realize now that it had its down side, too."

Like Timothy and many other young people, Linda needed the approval of her father. She wanted him to recognize the qualities in herself that she thought were special — her sensitivity and gift for art. Instead, her father expected her to follow the path to business success that he had prepared with years of hard work. His dream was to work alongside his daughter in the family business. He thought Linda's dreams of becoming an artist were unrealistic, the fleeting fantasies of youth. Her attacks on his adopted country and its government dismayed him, making him, if anything, more authoritarian and rigid in his responses to her.

Linda's father became the focal point of all her personal dissatisfactions and frustrations. This prevented her from dealing with her basic insecurities about herself. The conflict with her father became imbued with the "cover" of a legitimate but convoluted rationale. That is, nothing else was discussed, and both played out the drama without stopping to examine the possible real causes, such as questions about themselves. It was easier for each to see the other as the agent provocateur—the source of all the trouble.

In her arguments with her father, Linda felt she won the tacit approval of her mother, who over the years had conveyed her disapproval of Ernest with raised eyebrows, shrugs, and sighs. In this way, her teen-aged daughter became the repository of much of the antagonism Sonja herself felt but was incapable of expressing verbally. As Linda was drawn closer to her mother in an alliance against Ernest, the mutual disappointment of father and daughter increased. And the more she felt her father's disapproval and need to mold her in his own image, the more she tried to antagonize him, to prove to him that she was right and he was wrong. She couldn't see that behind the stubborn exterior of the man at the head of the table was a father who loved her deeply in his own way.

Verbal battles turned into open rebellion in Linda's late teens. She stayed out late at night, wore hippie clothes, and pasted leftist slogans on her bedroom wall. Teachers and other authority figures often received a knee-jerk response from her, and her choice of boyfriends seemed to be based on whether her father would disapprove of them. The scruffier and older they were, the better. "Usually I didn't have anything in common with the guys I dated. I probably chose them for their shock value. I certainly didn't have any satisfying sexual relationships. I saw myself as a free spirit, someone who would never be tied down, anyway not to a job like my father had. I had a girlfriend whose father, I thought, was the most wonderful dad in the world. He was easy to talk to, never pushed his views on us. He never wore a boring business suit. I wanted my dad to be more like him."

Toward the end of Linda's senior year, Sonja became alarmed by the intensity of the battles between father and daughter. Even Mara and Philip had begun to complain bitterly about the constant bickering and tension in the house. In an attempt to solve her family's problems, Sonja arranged a meeting with a family counselor. At the first session, the younger siblings said they disliked their father's authoritarian stance toward Linda, but also recounted examples of Linda's needling their father in a manner guaranteed to provoke one of his outbursts. Ernest felt besieged by everyone, and the overwhelmed young therapist spent the entire hour trying to rein everyone in, to no avail. Neither Linda nor her father were ready to make amends and both vowed never to return.

Linda believed her problems would be solved if she could get away from her family, her father in particular. She told herself that her questions about her own self-worth were caused by her father's criticisms. Once on her own, her increasingly unhappy moods would lift completely, or so she thought. During high school, she had saved a few thousand dollars from summer and part-time jobs. She had intended to use the money for college expenses, but had recently decided on a different plan. At the dinner table later that week, Linda shocked her family by announcing that after graduation the following month, she was going to fly to Europe, for an extended period, by herself.

Heading for a Fall

"I was so excited when I got on that plane. I'd done it. I'd left. I did feel bad about my mom because she was worried about a teen-ager traveling alone in Europe, but I felt that I'd finally shown my father that I could be my own person. He was furious. I think he even threatened to cut me off from the family. I didn't care. I was nineteen and my life was just beginning."

Like thousands of North American children from another generation, Linda was convinced that she would find her true self across the ocean in another land. Although she had never been religious — she attended synagogue with her family only on the High Holidays — she had always taken an interest in astrology and psychic powers. She believed that her flight from her family was predestined and that the plan of her future life would be revealed during her trip. She didn't have to wait long.

Many kids who are traveling alone for the first time with no particular destination look vulnerable and a bit confused when they first land in a foreign country. Linda was no exception. As she looked for her knapsack at the baggage claim at Orly Airport in Paris, she was spotted by a group of young people about her age who were waiting to pick up their baggage in the same area. A few left the group, introduced themselves, and asked where she was headed. "They all seemed to speak English. I remember thinking they were the friendliest, happiest people I'd ever met. I connected with them right away."

The young people in the group were from all over the world — the United States, England, Israel, Denmark, West Germany, and France. They were traveling by van to a farm in the Basque area of Spain, where their leader was based. At Orly, they were meeting a couple of kids who had arranged to be picked up there, but they had also learned that transit points were excellent places to recruit new members. In the past six months at train stations and airports, the original five members had convinced a dozen more to join them.

Eva, a soft-spoken girl with a mass of curly blond hair, was particularly persuasive as she talked to Linda about the group. She emphasized that although they weren't a religious group, they did have a mission. Their leader, a

Danish man called Hans, was a visionary whose ideas would change the world. Eva's hazel eyes never left Linda's brown ones as she described this wise man whose "March for Peace" would lead them through Europe, down through Turkey, Syria, and Lebanon, and finally into Jerusalem. Along the way, they would attract hundreds, perhaps thousands, of followers and, of course, the interest of the media. The entire world would then become aware of Hans and his message of peace. Best of all, Linda could be a part of it.

At first, Linda wasn't sure that she wanted to be a part of it. "I felt like everything was happening too fast. I mean, here were these kids I didn't even know asking me to go and live with them on a farm somewhere. . . . But they looked okay. They were all dressed just like me. They weren't druggies or anything and none of the guys were coming on to me. . . . I really liked the way they talked, too. They were so sure about what they were doing but, you know, in a serene kind of way." Belonging to a group of people who held similar ideals to her own was very appealing to Linda. Although she wouldn't have admitted it to anyone at that time, traveling with other people rather than on her own was also a plus. She decided to join them.

On their arrival at the farm, which belonged to a wealthy follower of Hans's, Linda congratulated herself on her good judgment. The vans stopped in front of a large vine-covered house surrounded by gently rolling fields. As they started to unload their luggage, the front door of the house was flung open and a short, sandy-haired young man strode out to embrace old followers and new. "He had the most amazing blue eyes I'd ever seen and this great smile. Right from the beginning he made me feel that I was meant to be there, that I was important to him and to the group."

For a city girl, Linda adapted quickly to life on a farm. Although local Basque farm workers did the bulk of the

planting, harvesting, and looking after the dairy, the commune members were expected to work in the vegetable
garden, tend the livestock, prepare meals, and do laundry.
To Linda, working hard with other people for a purpose that
she believed in was a highly satisfying way to live. Now
when she sat down to a meal, she felt a sense of belonging
that she hadn't felt for a long time at home.

The communal meals were eaten at a long, nineteenth-
century nunnery table. The women, by and large, worked in
the kitchen and cooked and served the meals. Hans, not
surprisingly, ruled his little flock from the head of the table.
The conversation was always animated, although every
member was careful to be deferential to their leader. When
he spoke, there was absolute silence. After the evening meal
was over, candles were lit and everyone joined hands and
sang "We Shall Overcome" and other well-known folk
songs. Each part of the day had similar small rituals. Doing
the same things at the same time every day — whether
saying prayers, singing, or doing calisthenics — provides a
predictable structure in a cult and has the effect of removing
ambiguity in one's life. Linda followed these rituals carefully
because it was expected of her but, more importantly,
because they made her feel safe.

The illusion of safety was destroyed two months later.
Shortly after she had arrived at the commune, Hans began
to take a special interest in the new girl from America —
asking her to sit beside him at meals, making eye contact
with her whenever he was speaking to the group, assigning
her tasks that he knew she liked, and spending more time
with her than the others. It didn't take long for Linda to fall
in love with this charismatic older man and to find herself
sharing his bed. Her belief in their love and life together
absorbed her thoughts to the exclusion of everything else.
Because Hans had indoctrinated his followers against their

parents and former life styles, she was already not writing regularly to her family; soon she even forgot their birthdays.

Back home, Ernest and Sonja were worried that they were losing their daughter. Linda's earlier letters, full of "light and love and dedication to the cause," had set off warning bells. Sonja visited the local library and gathered as much information as she could on cults. From what she read, she decided that their best course of action was to try and keep in touch with Linda to show her that they still cared and that she was still a part of their family. For a while, Ernest talked about kidnapping his wayward child and bringing her home to be deprogrammed. Sonja, on the other hand, had read enough to know that this extreme measure rarely helps children involved in cults. She also knew her husband well enough to realize that, in the end, he wouldn't be able to participate in something illegal. All they could do at this point, because the phone was disconnected at the farm, was to write frequently, and hope that at least some of the letters got through (some did).

Her new relationship with Hans automatically granted Linda a certain status in the commune. The fact that her new family, particularly the displaced Eva, resented her position didn't bother her. The only relationship that truly mattered to her was the one she had with Hans. This was a new attitude for her. Previously, her like-minded girlfriends had been more important to her than her boyfriends. "I felt that in the seven weeks I had been away from home, I had found everything I wanted in life — love, passion, status, important work that would help the world, a great place to live . . . everything. I felt like it was preordained somehow. And it didn't matter to me that some people resented me. I thought that would change eventually. Actually, I didn't really care if it did or not. I just wandered around in this blissful little bubble."

Even when Hans revealed his flaws — and there were a number of them — Linda found excuses for them rather than admitting that this godlike man wasn't perfect. She discovered, for example, that he wouldn't listen to anyone else's opinion, particularly if the person talking happened to be a woman. As long as Linda agreed with him and played handmaiden to him, he was satisfied. However, when she did voice an opinion, he would either ignore her or reply sarcastically. At times he would become verbally abusive. She convinced herself that such reactions were simply a result of his being preoccupied with more important matters. Love for Linda wasn't only blind, it was deaf as well.

When Linda became pregnant, she was ecstatic. She remembers returning from the doctor's and lying in the middle of a sunny field, feeling a part of all the growing things around her, planning how to tell Hans, imagining what their child would look like. Caught up in her mystical view of life, practical considerations never entered her mind. That afternoon she put on Hans's favorite dress and arranged to meet him in their bedroom, which she had decorated with bouquets of wild flowers. Hans was wary as soon as he entered the room. Instead of the shared joy she had expected, he reacted to her news with rage. After repeatedly calling her a stupid fool, he swept a vase of flowers from a table and abruptly left the room. What followed was a bewilderingly rapid sequence of events that Linda even now has difficulty recounting.

It began that evening. Hans wandered in after everyone else had sat down for the evening meal. He had obviously been drinking. He stood at the end of the table accusing her of fantasizing about his love for her, of being a naïve little child. He then denounced the entire group, saying that they weren't worthy of him and that he was returning to his wife and children in Denmark. No one knew that he was married with a family, least of all Linda. The next day he stuffed his clothing into a back pack and left. "I couldn't understand it. I thought we had this magical relationship, I thought he loved me, I thought we had this mission together. I couldn't believe that he would leave me, especially when I was carrying his child, but I couldn't do anything to stop him. I was totally helpless. The bastard didn't leave me any money. He didn't even leave an address."

Hitting Rock Bottom

In a very short period of time, Linda's new-found self-esteem, sense of belonging, and belief system had been destroyed. Her sense of hurt and betrayal were overwhelming. She had cut herself off from her own family and the members of her new one, leaving her with no one to turn to for guidance or help. Shut up in the bedroom that had held only happy memories until a few days ago, she curled up in a rocking chair and cried. She couldn't sleep or eat and soon began to lose touch with reality. She didn't know where she was or indeed who she was. Although the other commune members were also suffering from the shock of their leader's leaving, they recognized that Linda needed help. Two of the older members packed her clothes and drove her into France and then on to Paris. They took her to an old hospital on the outskirts of the city, where they led her into the Emergency Room and then abruptly left. All Linda remembers of that day is that she badly wanted to die.

It was clear to the medical and nursing staff in the rural hospital that Linda was very confused and frightened. However, none of them on duty that day spoke English well enough to take an accurate history, and Linda was in no shape to give one in her broken high-school French. Even had she been able, would they have believed her bizarre tale? Because she looked so disheveled and seemed so disorganized, they thought at first that she was on psychedelic drugs. When the drug screen came back negative, they decided that her age and symptoms were at least consistent with a first schizophrenic breakdown. She was tentatively diagnosed as having acute undifferentiated schizophrenia, a serious mental illness, and placed in the Inpatient Psychiatry Unit.

What Linda in fact was experiencing was what the public refers to as a nervous breakdown. If you force any kind of machine to perform beyond its capabilities, it will start to break down. The same is true of people. Linda's mind simply couldn't process the information it was being given. People can handle a crisis if it's expected or if they can make some sense out of it; too many thoughts that they can't make sense of can lead to slow reflexes, an inability to eat or sleep, and erratic behavior.

Linda was taken to a large, bare room with a yellowing linoleum floor and four white-painted iron beds. A barred window overlooked a small courtyard filled with cars. There were three other women in the room — one her own age and two women in their sixties. They tried to speak to her as best they could in English, but she was too depressed to make the effort to reply. The language barrier also prevented the elderly psychiatrist who ran the ward from finding out much about her other than her age. A brusque, somewhat preoccupied man, he seemed to have made up his mind about her problem after a quick glance at the chart that had been filled out in the Emergency Room. He prescribed a major tranquilizer called chlorpromazine, an anti-psychotic medication. No one had asked the young foreigner if she was pregnant. If the hospital staff had known, it is unlikely that such a drug would have been prescribed.

Intuitively, Linda felt she shouldn't take the pills. "I don't think I trusted anybody then. My baby was all I had left. I didn't want anything to hurt her, so I pretended to take the pills and then I'd hide them in the pocket of my skirt." After four days in the unit with little attention from the staff, Linda's mounting fear and despair forced her to take some action on her own behalf. She managed to convey to a nurse that she wanted to call her parents. At the nurses' station, as she watched one of the nurses dial her home number, she began to cry. By the time both parents got on the line, about all they could understand from the brief sentences between sobs was that Linda was hospitalized, pregnant, alone, and seemingly out of control. Ernest, hopelessly confused about what had happened to his daughter and what action he should take, told Linda to listen to the doctor and nurses and he would call her back soon.

Linda had hoped to be rescued from the hospital full of strangers she couldn't understand and from the emptiness and fear she felt inside. Instead, she hung up the phone feeling rejected by her father once more. "I wasn't sure he would call again, and I knew Mom would go along with whatever he decided to do. I'd made this mess of my life and I thought no one was going to save me. I didn't really think I was worth saving at that point anyway."

Lying on her bed in the psychiatric ward, Linda lost all hope. She had reached that critical period we all reach in a crisis and she chose death over life. With shaking hands, she gathered up the pills she had been hiding, took the juice from the supper tray, climbed into bed, and drew the curtains around her. People about to kill themselves often think with a strange logic. In Linda's case, she chose juice rather than water because she was still thinking about the health of her unborn child. Even as she gulped down the tiny yellow and blue pills that she had refused to take before, she thought about her child. She planned to ring the nurse as soon as she felt herself losing consciousness, thinking that her baby might have a chance to be saved. Her main thought, however, was to end her own life as quickly as possible.

When she began to get sleepy, Linda did in fact manage to ring for a nurse. The hospital staff immediately sprang into action, using a variety of medical techniques to rid Linda's body of the drugs she had ingested and to make sure she didn't slip into a coma.

Linda awoke to find her parents sitting beside her bed. She was shocked to be alive but even more astounded that her parents were there with her. Her father's face was wet with tears. It was the first time she had ever seen him cry and the first time she had known deep within herself that he loved her. She couldn't speak because her throat was so sore from the nasogastric tube, but her tentative smile was enough to reassure Ernest and Sonja. When they left for their hotel that evening, Linda began to question her own actions and emotions in a way that was new for her. "I remember wondering how I could have hated my father who obviously loved me but fallen in love with Hans who used me and didn't care at all. I was trying to understand how I could have been so blind about so many things. I decided that I hadn't really meant to kill myself, that I just wanted some-one — my father, I guess — to help me or love me or whatever, just so that I wouldn't be alone in the world. I had this incredibly strong feeling that I wanted to live but in a different way."

Linda recovered quickly from the physical trauma of her overdose and resuscitation. A few days later, she flew home with her parents. Although returning home was comforting, after a while some of her old negative feelings about her father began to resurface. "I felt like he was smothering me — asking too many questions, expecting answers I didn't have." The return of such feelings is to be expected. The moment of clarity that we may experience after a crisis is like opening a door into our new home within, but we aren't able to step over the threshold yet; old patterns in our relationships with people close to us or circumstances in our lives hold us back. In Linda's case, relief at not being in the hospital turned to self-pity as she reflected on her predicament — four months pregnant, unmarried, no education, no job, and no place of her own to live. At her parents' urging, she came to see me.

New Beginnings

The young woman I met looked like a bewildered waif. She had obviously been crying for days. Although she still presented herself as a sixties' flower child, the rhetoric that she had believed in for the last few years was now irrelevant. The fact was that she was going to give birth in five months and was totally unprepared. She hadn't recovered from the abandonment by her lover or her suicide attempt and was confused about where she belonged in the world. Her parents were unable to help, and her friends from school, although sympathetic, had a hard time understanding how she had gotten into the mess that she was in. Like all of us who are at a crisis point in our lives, she needed to talk to someone objective.

In a tremulous voice and with tear-filled eyes, she told me her story. I thought as we talked that no young person should have to make the kind of decisions that Linda had to make at that time. Too late for a therapeutic abortion, she had to decide between keeping her baby or giving it up for adoption. In the best of circumstances this is a difficult situation. In one where the mother's partner has deserted her and suicide has been attempted, it is doubly so. Linda had tried to put the problem out of her mind but of course she couldn't, and this played a major role in her increasing despondency. This was yet another situation in which she felt powerless. Before a rapidly approaching deadline, she had to answer a number of questions. If she kept the child, where would she live and how would she support herself? If she chose adoption, how would she arrange it and who would the adoptive parents be?

The first step in our work together was to ensure that Linda saw a counselor in family planning, someone who didn't have prior opinions about keeping or giving up a child, who would have Linda's best interests at heart, and who would let her make her own decision once she had been given all the information she needed to make that decision. The counselor suggested that she talk to some young single mothers who had kept their children and to some teen-age mothers whose babies had been adopted. Linda found these informal meetings set up by her counselor particularly helpful. "I liked being able to talk to women my own age. Their experiences were real. I could relate to them. It gave me a sense of what my own life would be like if I kept the baby and if I didn't."

Ernest and Sonja wanted their daughter to give the baby up. Predictably, Linda's first reaction was to keep the child because her parents wanted her to do the opposite. In time, though, as she worked through her own needs, she changed her mind. She desperately wanted to go back to school, as a way of leaving the past behind and ensuring an independent life for herself. She also began to consider her parents' needs at this stage in their lives. Those needs didn't include looking after a grown daughter and a newborn. With the help of her counselor, she arranged to have the baby adopted by a young Jewish couple who had been unable to have children of their own. Although she didn't meet them, she wrote to them, enclosing a long letter to be given to her child later in life.

When her daughter was born, her joy at giving birth to a healthy, beautiful baby was quickly followed by grief. Giving up her child was the final, and certainly the most devastating, loss for this young woman. The baby represented her only link with the man whom she still loved despite his cruel rejection of her. For a long while thereafter, each baby Linda saw reminded her of her own. Sometimes her inner torment would become overwhelming, and she would desperately want to escape from herself and the circumstances that imprisoned her. These thoughts were terrifying because they reminded her of her previous breakdown.

Linda's fears at this time were not unusual. Once having undergone a serious clinical depression, even waking up in a bad mood will sometimes set off an "Oh my God, here I go again" type of reaction. It can take a few years for the mood swings of everyday life to be seen as just that — a normal occurrence. Although the hurt Linda felt at this time equaled the hurt she had felt at Hans's betrayal, she had become stronger since her return home. She had people now to help her when life was too difficult to handle on her own, and she had rediscovered her faith.

Although Linda had dabbled in astrology and mysticism, she didn't turn to these in her recovery. They hadn't served her particularly well in the past year. Instead, she turned to her childhood religion. Partly she did this out of a need to define herself in a spiritual way —What am I now going to believe in? — and partly it was a reaching out for help in another direction. For a few months, she joined an ultra Orthodox Jewish synagogue, where she found herself swept up in the same kind of intense fervor that she had experienced in the commune in Spain. "I eventually had this sense of déjà vu and decided to slow down and take a good look at what I was becoming involved in before committing myself further." This was a welcome sign of a growing maturity.

Linda enrolled in college, moved out, and found a part-time job teaching art to children at a recreation center. The busier she became with school, job, and extracurricular activities, the less time she had to think about the losses in her life. She was now clearly moving forward. There were a few setbacks. She had a couple of relationships with men, but the scars from her experience with Hans hadn't healed, and the relationships didn't last. The two key men in her life, her father and Hans, had made her extremely wary of the opposite sex. She needed to believe that all men weren't alike and she needed to confront her role in causing some of the problems that she had had with Hans and her father. In her relationship with Ernest, she finally accepted that he wasn't going to change and that there were parts of him that she loved and parts she couldn't stand. She also admitted to herself that she didn't have all the answers either and that some of their problems had been as much her fault as his.

Sonja and Ernest's marriage broke apart in the period when Linda went back to school. After Linda left, Sonja took ownership of her own feelings and decided she wanted a divorce. Although she is leading a full, active life, Ernest is a bitter, angry man. Linda sees him from time to time for dinner and regrets that he has in some ways been abandoned by the rest of the family. In his own crisis, she helps him as best she can, realizing from her own experience how little she can do until he is willing to help himself.

Five Years Later

As Linda committed herself to changing her life for the better, the drive that had always been a part of her personality became focused on personal growth rather than looking for magical answers or disparaging her father or the "system." Three years later, the bewildered little girl had become a self-confident adult. Today Linda has a Masters in Arts and Humanities, teaches art at a local college, paints and sculpts, and is seriously involved with a young co-worker, whom she tells me is decidedly non-mystical and non-charismatic.

4. Measuring Up and Failing

"I *NEVER* FORGET AN INSULT," SHE SAID, looking at me defiantly through a pair of old-fashioned glasses, her face fringed with lank brown hair. She mentioned this fact about herself with a great deal of pride, the way certain people slap you on the back and crow, "I never forget a face." This rather dubious ability and her obvious intelligence were the two attributes that Anna Younis mentioned when pressed to explore what she liked about herself. There was nothing else.

Her parents, Nick and Helen, would probably say that their eldest daughter had been born with a chip on her shoulder. As a baby, she had been colicky and much more demanding than her elder brother, Gregory, and her younger sister, Maria. Helen attributed this to the fact that Anna was adopted. After eight years of trying to conceive after the birth of their son, she and Nick had arranged a private adoption of a baby girl. Then, as seems to happen so often, Maria was born seven months after Anna was brought home.

As a child, Anna managed quite well. She had a brilliant mind, her teachers were supportive, and her sharp tongue and witty remarks endeared her to a few like-minded friends. Her parents seemed to accept her rather sour disposition, perhaps reasoning that it must be difficult having a popular sister who was almost the same age and an older brother who showed little interest in her. Gregory's friends and extracurricular activities meant that he was away from home a great deal, but when he was home, it was clear to Anna where his affections lay. He doted on Maria, a warm-hearted, attractive girl with a winning personality. The sisters could not have been more dissimilar. Maria naturally attracted people of all ages to her, while Anna tended to alienate them. Still, Anna did so well in school and Maria so poorly that she had a strong sense of pride in her own achievements.

In high school, Anna's interpersonal problems began to escalate. Hormonal changes and social pressure take their toll on many teen-agers; however, Anna seemed to be irritable all the time. She repeatedly compared herself to Maria. "Maria couldn't do anything wrong. I used to think, well, what do you expect, Anna? She's the real daughter, not you. In high school, she was one of those bimbo cheerleaders. Of course, all my family thought that was fantastic. It didn't matter that she was failing her exams." Life with this sullen young girl was a life of walking on eggshells. At school, most of her friends managed to hurt her feelings in some way and were dropped. With Julia and Pam, her two remaining chums, she could be the witty friend of old, but they too were careful about what they said around her. At home, Nick and Helen tried to make their daughter feel loved and wanted, but she continued to be either withdrawn or combative.

We've all met teen-agers like Anna. Nothing is ever their fault, always someone else's. When they come from a middle-class background and have parents who love them, we often have little patience for their complaints. We want to say, "Lighten up," "Be thankful for what you have," "Do something about your problems." It's often difficult to see the shy, scared individuals behind the angry facades. These children are the way they are because they're caught in a circle of rejection. The more they crave but do not receive affection from others, the more closed and self-protective their behavior becomes, which in turn alienates people even more. This circle can begin very early in life. As young children, if people respond to us more coolly than to other children because we are less attractive or more difficult to care for, we are given a clear but subtle message that we are less desirable. We learn early in life to reject ourselves.

Heading for a Fall

Anna saw rejection wherever she looked. Her myth about herself was that she was unattractive and unwanted. At seventeen, when she developed a severe case of facial and body acne, her self-esteem plummeted. She had never had a date and now believed that she never would, particularly after some insensitive boys in her class began to tease her about her appearance. When the lesions began to ulcerate and bleed, she was hospitalized for three months and placed on heavy doses of medication, including steroids. Used to treat a variety of severe disorders, steroids can have a number of unpleasant side effects. In Anna's case, they caused a significant weight gain, which further damaged her self-image.

At home that summer, she lay for a little while each day on a blanket in the back yard, letting the sun help heal her damaged skin. When her sister's friends drove up the driveway to pick up Maria, Anna would scurry around to the side of the house until they disappeared. "Why would I want them to see me? I looked repulsive. They always looked like they'd just walked out of a magazine. Can you imagine the looks on their faces if they'd seen me — the blob on the blanket?" Maria invited her along from time to time, but after a steady stream of refusals, the entire family stopped trying to include her in their summer plans. By the time fall arrived, her acne scars had faded significantly to all eyes but Anna's. "You would have had to have been blind not to see them. My mother and sister kept telling me they weren't noticeable but I knew they were. I knew they were lying to me. I wasn't stupid! I could see what I looked like! They didn't understand. I didn't want their pity. I just wanted to be left alone."

She got her wish. Julia and Pam had telephoned or visited several times during the holidays, only to be met with the same refusals to go anywhere that Anna's family had grown accustomed to. The unhappy truth was that the sight of her two healthy friends leading normal lives — both now had boyfriends — filled her with envy. She didn't want to hear about their boyfriends or the school gossip about who was going out with whom. She didn't want to go shopping or swimming or camping. She *couldn't*. Like other teen-aged girls, she believed the popular media's message that you must be thin and beautiful to be desirable. This strong belief that her appearance would prevent her from ever being a participant in the carefree life that her friends enjoyed was a frightening thought, one she felt powerless to change. As

her fear and pessimism grew, Anna became openly antagonistic toward everyone. Anger became a way to defend
herself against the rejection she expected from the world.
Soon even her two friends were unwilling to put up with her
constant criticism and dark view of life.

In the fall, she began university. The days quickly settled
into a routine that Anna rarely changed. She went to lectures in the morning, quickly ate lunch in an empty classroom or washroom rather than face the other students in
the cafeteria, attended lectures or labs in the afternoon,
took the bus home, ate dinner, and locked herself in her
room to study. Her achievements in her science course
were admired by her peers, but her standoffish demeanor
and caustic remarks didn't make them want to know her any
better. She remained friendless.

In her final year of university, the acne returned, not as
severely this time, but enough to terrify her. Again, the
lesions healed and again Anna was unable to see that she was
actually quite attractive. Instead, she adopted a "what the
hell" attitude. It wasn't unusual for her to go off to school
with her hair unwashed and uncombed, clothes wrinkled,
and nails dirty. Her entire approach to life was "why
bother?"

Although Anna wasn't hospitalized during this bout of her
illness, she did miss many classes and saw her original
dreams of professional or graduate school disappear. Needless to say, her graduation day was not a happy one. Much to
her parents' dismay, she refused to go to the ceremony or
have her graduation portrait taken. "I couldn't understand
why they thought I should go to commencement or have my
picture taken. I was a failure. Without a post-graduate
degree, I'd just end up washing beakers in some lab. I didn't

have any friends to party with. What was there to celebrate?" That summer she began to live in a fortress of self-
hatred. No one was allowed in and Anna wasn't allowed out.

Hitting Rock Bottom

Like Timothy, Anna slipped into what is known as a clinical
depression. She would wake up at three or four in the
morning and not be able to get back to sleep. During the day
she felt incapable of doing anything more than consuming
large quantities of food, a common response to stress.
Gradually she became housebound physically inside her
parents' home and mentally inside herself.

Her sadness, self-recrimination, and rage against the
world finally erupted one evening as her mother tried to
reach out and help her. Between sobs, she told Helen that
she now thought the only way out of her problems was to kill
herself. "I remember saying that some people are born
blessed like Maria, and then there are people like me who
are cursed right from the start." Alarmed by the conviction
in her daughter's voice, Helen called the family doctor who
suggested that she take Anna to the local hospital. After a
great deal of persuasion, Anna agreed to go and was admitted into the short-stay crisis unit for seventy-two hours of
observation. She was placed on anti-depressant medication
and discharged after two days, partly because she was so
hostile, partly because the staff didn't think she would kill
herself, and partly because of the shortage of beds in the
unit.

Before she left the hospital, Anna was given an appointment to a follow-up clinic and a prescription for the anti-
depressant she had been taking. Unfortunately, no one gave
her any information about the medication. At home, the

drug didn't make her feel any better even after a week. "I was tired all the time. I felt stoned, completely out of it, so I stopped taking the pills." To have any effect, most anti-depressants must be taken for a minimum of two weeks. Keeping her appointment at the clinic was also dismissed. "There was no way I was going to sit in a waiting room with a bunch of crazy people."

Her thoughts of suicide remained with her. Unlike Timothy and Linda, though, suicide for Anna was seen as a way of hurting other people as well as ending her suffering. She imagined gruesome ways of killing herself that would shock everyone she knew, making them pay for her death with the remorse that she felt she had been saddled with for years. If not for her intense anger, her sense of powerlessness might have led to suicide. As it was, the lashing out at everyone around her who she felt contributed to her misery was enough to keep her "alive," even though the word had a very restricted meaning at that time in her life.

Nick and Helen had explored every avenue to help their daughter. They pointed out jobs in the newspaper that they thought she might be qualified for. Her mother tried to persuade her to see a therapist. They both tried to placate her when she turned on them. Her mild-mannered, confused father had even given her a car in an attempt to show how much he loved her. (Her brother and sister had never had one bought for them.) In a subtle way, however, all their bending-over-backward attempts gave Anna a very different message than the one they were trying to convey. The message was that she was different; she couldn't make it on her own.

One Saturday morning, Gregory, who was now thirty and living on his own in another city, was visiting for the weekend. A big, placid man like his father, he was present when Anna unleashed one of her verbal attacks on her parents.

There was silence and then Gregory for the first time told his sister what he thought of her. "He said he was tired of being told that he should feel sorry for me, that I was spoiled rotten, a selfish bitch, and a loser. My parents didn't say a word." Anna stormed out of the house. By the time Helen reached the door to try and stop her, her daughter was in her car and on her way to a local shopping mall.

Still furious with her family, she began to wander aimlessly around a large department store, picking things up and putting them down. At the gloves counter, she suddenly remembered that she did in fact need a pair and asked the young salesgirl to find her size for her. When she asked Anna to wait while she finished helping another customer, Anna's belief that the whole world was out to get her and her jealousy of anyone who was attractive produced a stream of insults directed at the hapless clerk. The clerk's "I'm sorry, madam, you'll have to wait" produced another loud barrage of profanity. When an elderly saleswoman took her arm to get her attention, Anna reacted with such hostility that she accidentally knocked the poor woman to the floor. A security guard was called, followed shortly by the police, who drove Anna to the same hospital she had been taken to before.

On the trip to the hospital in the squad car, Anna felt humiliated and ashamed. "I'd completely lost control over a pair of gloves I didn't even particularly like. It was like something out of a bad movie." Fortunately, no charges were laid, and by the time she had finished talking to a social worker in the Emergency Room, her entire family had arrived to pick her up. Despite this experience and her family's show of support, Anna continued on her destructive path. She continued to blame others for not recognizing that she had a far worse time of it than anyone else and now attributed all of her problems to her appearance. She was literally unable to look in the mirror and see that she was a pleasant-looking person. All she saw was ugliness inflicted by a cruel God.

Like Gregory, Nick Younis's compassion for his daughter had all but evaporated. "I think Mom thought I might still kill myself so she didn't say anything to me, but I guess Dad had reached the end of his rope." After yet another of his daughter's displays of misery mixed with insults, he told her angrily that she had always been difficult to live with and that it had nothing to do with her skin problems. "I'd never seen him so mad. It was unbelievable. But what really got to me was he said I should see a psychiatrist." For Anna, this was as great an insult as she could imagine coming from her father. Like Linda's father, Nick was an immigrant who had had no help in starting up his restaurant business. He had often said that people should be able to stand on their own two feet without the help of mollycoddling "shrinks." For him to suggest that she see one filled Anna with rage. Again she ran out of the house. This time, nobody followed her.

Anna got in her car and began to drive; it didn't matter where as long as it was away from her family. She turned onto a highway that led out of the city and began racing through the darkness as fast as she could. "The police clocked me at a hundred miles an hour. When they finally stopped me, the cop that came to the window at first thought I might have been drinking. But when he saw I hadn't been, he wanted to know what I thought I was doing." The concerned look on the officer's face and the tone of his voice stopped the flow of rage that had dominated her confused thoughts from the time she had left the house. She placed the speeding ticket in her purse, rolled up the window, and drove slowly to the next exit ramp. After parking the car on a deserted side road, she began to ask herself the policeman's question — what *was* she doing with her life and to the people she loved? She realized she couldn't go on living the way she had been; feeling a wonderful sense of release from her anger and despair, she decided to start a new life.

When Anna reached home five hours later, her worried parents met her at the door. They were prepared for more angry words; instead, their daughter began to cry and clung to each of them in turn. It had been a long time since Anna had wanted to be held by Nick and Helen. Without blaming anyone but herself, she told them how unhappy she was with her life and how she now knew that she needed help. This critical point was Anna's "moment of truth." There was no other way to go but up.

New Beginnings

Anna had reached a crucial point. She was committed to changing her life, but between that commitment and the actual steps that had to be taken lay fear and some ambivalence. To change old patterns of behavior at a time when a person is feeling emotionally depleted is a difficult task. Although Anna knew she needed help, it had never been easy for her to open up to another person. She dreaded going to a mental health professional. Her skepticism about the benefits of therapy also prevented her from picking up the phone and making an appointment. Finally, after days of procrastination, she found the courage to phone a psychiatrist that her family doctor had recommended.

"It was a disaster. No offense, but this guy confirmed all my worst fears about going into therapy. I told him about my problems but he didn't seem to have any advice. He just sat there nodding his head. I thought if I'm not crazy already, this man's going to drive me crazy." Sometimes therapists and their patients don't click, and unfortunately, this is what happened to Anna. If a person doesn't feel comfortable with his or her therapist, it's a good idea to raise the issue in a session. Most therapists are humble enough to accept that they may not be right for every job. In this situation, they will simply refer a patient to someone else. Anna, on the other hand, took a different route and found my name in a directory of women's services.

The old Anna would have rejected all therapy after one negative experience. At the age of twenty-seven, however, she was ready to tear down her fortress and build an inner home. It wasn't easy. Facing one's problems can involve a lot of pain before the healing process starts. In the beginning, she saw our weekly therapy sessions as a sign of failure and some of my questions as personal attacks. As we talked about her life and the role that anger and bitterness had played in it, she would sometimes become very antagonistic. She would insult me, attack my abilities, question my motives; some of her accusations hit home, but I could see through the verbal artillery a very scared child. That old pattern of hurting someone first before they could hurt her was difficult to change, but gradually she learned to trust me and began to make some real progress. Through her own inner work, she began to gain an understanding of the origins of her anger, her jealousy of her siblings, and her fear that her illness was a punishment for past behavior. She also explored the problems she had to deal with in the present and what she could do to change her life.

On a clear, cold Sunday morning, Anna found herself doing something that she would never have imagined herself doing the previous year. She went to the Greek Orthodox church that her family attended. After the service, she spoke to a warm, engaging priest whom she remembered from her childhood. He invited her into his office and she talked to him about her life. Now that the defensive walls that she had hidden behind had come down, Anna was finding that telling her story strengthened her resolve to admit her problems and solve them. The elderly priest realized that she needed to hear from him that she was on the right track. He also correctly surmised that she was looking for a spiritual presence in her life. He gave her the reassurance she needed and invited her to attend church services and to visit him whenever she wanted. "As a kid, I used to skip down the steps of that church. It was fun to do because there were so many of them. And that day I felt like doing it again. I felt that good."

The old adage that "there are no atheists in foxholes" is true. Most people in crisis think at some point of their relationship to God or to some spiritual presence. I have found that this phenomenon — belief in something greater than oneself — is a crucial element in the regeneration of one's life. Spirituality is in fact built into many treatment programs (especially the Twelve-Step programs). There is a certain comfort in knowing that there may be some "grand game plan," or that someone or something "up there" is in charge even if we aren't. Spirituality may then evolve from a passive "I will be cared for" to an active "How can I live up to my higher values and ideals?"

Anna's quest to discover her spiritual roots was followed by one to find her biological parents. In defining our identity, it is not only important to know who we are and where we are going, but also from where we came. She had many questions, which will be familiar to all adopted teen-agers and adults. What are my biological parents like? Why was I given away? Do I have any siblings? Am I the way I am because of a terrible background? In most jurisdictions, adoptees are now given information to enable them to find their birth parents. There are even private companies listed in the Yellow Pages that will assist in this process. However, because Anna had been privately adopted, there were no available public records. For once, luck seemed to be on Anna's side. The doctor who had arranged the adoption was able to give her enough information to trace her mother.

Understandably, she was very nervous about contacting her birth mother. Her fear of possible rejection kept her from calling for some time. In the past, Anna had made major decisions about her life on her own, or in recent years had simply languished at home unable to make any decisions at all. This time she didn't allow her uncertainty to linger. She talked to her parents, who were supportive although they had some reservations, and she discussed this step with me. None of us told her what to do. It was her decision and in the end she decided to call. She phoned Irena Kalikos, who was now Mrs. Irena Belanger, on a weekday morning. When Anna first identified herself, her mother began to cry then, quickly regaining her composure, suggested they meet for lunch the next day.

Not all meetings between birth parents and their children are as successful as the one between Anna and Irena was. Irena, an attractive, dark-haired, soft-spoken woman was an accountant and the mother of two teen-age girls. She had no idea where Anna's father was, but believed that he had moved to France long ago. "She was fifteen when she got pregnant. Obviously she couldn't keep me. She wanted to but they were just too young. When she heard from her doctor about my parents and how wonderful they were, she decided to give me up. No money changed hands, nothing like that. She said she'd thought about me a lot and wondered whether I was happy or not." It was important for Anna to know that she was a child who was conceived in love.

To her surprise, in response to Irena's questions, she found herself talking about the "up side" of her life — her academic achievements, her family, even plans for the future. It all spilled out in a very natural, spontaneous way. Nothing was contrived for Irena's benefit; she meant every word. They spent three hours talking and looking at photographs that Irena had brought of her family and, before they said good-bye, agreed to meet again in a few months. Anna finally felt that she "belonged."

When I saw Anna after this meeting with her natural mother, what she was most excited about were her responses to Irena's questions. She felt as though she had left the past behind. The bitterness she had felt toward her family had been replaced with love, and she was beginning to truly believe in herself and her abilities. She asked me what I thought about her going to medical school. "What do you think about it?" I asked. And, as if she had been thinking about this for a long time, which she had not consciously done, she laid out a plan for making up a couple of prerequisite courses in the fall and then applying to medical school.

Five Years Later

Five years later, Anna is in her final year of a unique medical school, which recruits people of unusual backgrounds and work experience. She and her family are on very good terms, and she has made friends and dates occasionally when time allows. Sometimes I hear from her when she needs a "jag of stability," as she calls it. I like to think that when she looks in the mirror now, she sees what I see in her face — an enthusiasm for life, a keen sense of humor, and a compassion for those in need.

Part Two

The Midlife Quest

Many people have referred to our time on earth as a journey. I also like to think of it as three circles, with the middle years overlapping both adolescence and the senior years. Psychologically, there are no rigid delineations between the ages. We've all met people who at forty act in ways that some of us might consider irreverent or irresponsible, or simply adolescent, and other people of the same age whom we might consider rigid, or narrow-thinking, or simply old before their time. Nevertheless, what we all share during this long span of time is a continuation of the tasks involved in our adolescent search for an inner home. In contrast to the teen-age years, however, these tasks are expanded in midlife and translated into behaviors and actions that are in keeping with added demands and responsibilities. Trying to fulfill the more attainable of our adolescent dreams characterizes midlife.

In the early middle years, in our twenties and thirties, we work on these tasks with great energy. We don't dream about independence from our parents; we are independent or are certainly attempting to be. We can no longer merely consider various career or job options; we must choose. Our circle of friends may change drastically as different life styles and careers are chosen. Many of us form intimate relationships and marry or live together. Others start families. Our self-esteem and sense of belonging are affected by each of these changes in our lives. Because we are concentrating on building a life for ourselves, many of us neglect our spiritual side at this age and get drawn into the myths of midlife.

In our achievement-oriented, competitive society, the most prevalent myth of this age group is the perceived necessity to "make it." For some of us, power, fame, and/or the acquisition of great sums of money and possessions become our overriding goal. The achievement of any of these so-called measures of success, though, rarely proves to be enough. There is always pressure to do more, produce more, accumulate more, and consume more. Life is reduced to the size of house, kind of car, and type of school, never one's intrinsic worth as a person. Even if the outer semblances of success seem to be there initially, the frenetic runners on this route know deep inside that their success is ephemeral. They feel fraudulent and empty.

One woman I know described how out of touch with the natural world around her she became at this stage in life. At the time, she and her husband owned a wonderful old cottage perched high up on a cliff overlooking an island-dotted lake. "When we first bought the property, I couldn't look at the cottage or the view without thinking how envious my friends would be when they saw it. I saw it completely through their eyes, and when I worked on it — painting or whatever — it was to improve it for them, not for me. It was only after my divorce and the sale of the cottage that I realized how much time I had wasted trying to keep up with other people and worrying about what they would think, when I could have been out paddling a canoe and feeding my soul on all that incredible beauty."

Many of the personal myths of midlife that prevent people from developing strong emotional foundations are formed in childhood. Some of these become more acute as a result of the success myth. There is a kind of double jeopardy involved. If you believe you are a failure or no good or without ability, you can end up feeling fragile and vulnerable when something goes wrong in the very years that you are supposed to be most productive. Men and women in this situation have the sense that their lives are under siege and about to collapse. This is particularly true of people in their forties, who sometimes feel this decade is their last chance to "make it."

One couple I know who are both in their early forties are a good example. This is a second marriage for each one. The wife has two children who live one week with her and one week with their father. The husband has visitation rights to his child. In addition to grumbling about these complicated family arrangements, both feel they aren't where they want to be in their careers and both have money worries. In the past few months, he has had bronchial pneumonia, problems with an old shoulder injury, and recently broke his arm skating. She suffers from migraine headaches and recently injured her leg after tripping over a toy. He smokes, she overeats. "We just can't seem to get our act together," she complains. "Once everything settles down a bit, I'm going to do something about it."

I have to smile whenever people tell me they will take steps to change the way they are living as soon as "things settle down." It seldom, if ever, happens. Life in our fast-paced world has a way of throwing new zingers at us all the time — deadlines, illness, financial problems. What often happens is that people attempt to escape from facing their difficulties through alcohol, drugs, overwork, or promiscuity. Sometimes these are part and parcel of the success myth. This becomes readily apparent when you consider the business and entertainment figures of the past few years who have lost everything at this stage of their lives. Instead of helping us, these destructive escapes become problems in themselves.

Another way to avoid facing our own deficiencies and solving them is to find a complementary partner who can help plug those holes for us. Many people get married at a young age hoping for some magical sense of fulfillment from their new husband or wife. In effect, they are looking for someone to complete them. Instead, they should be looking for ways to fulfill themselves personally, socially, and spiritually. Waiting for someone else to do it for us is almost always doomed to failure and puts an enormous strain on a relationship.

In addition to the pressures of living with another person, one of the biggest challenges of this age group is beginning a family. The arrival of children is exciting, but it also signals the true end of adolescent freedom and the beginning of a lifelong commitment. Our lives become issue-laden — Should one of us stay at home with the baby or should we choose day care? What kind of day care? Should we bottlefeed or breastfeed? Should we live in the city or move to the country? Because everything has an unfamiliar air of seriousness about it, we can easily feel out of our depth and burdened. Individuals with inner and outer support systems in place can cope quite well with this onslaught of new experiences and feelings, but those without have particular difficulty.

During the transition between the middle years and later years, we begin to think about aging and its implications. It is the paradox of these years that just at the point we feel we "have it made" socially, or professionally, or monetarily, our bodies begin to fail us. We begin to realize we can no longer compete as athletically as we once did. Some of us worry that we can no longer perform as well mentally, either. Unlike adolescents, we begin to accept that our lives are not going to go on forever. With these thoughts comes a search for spiritual answers and sometimes a great fear of death, which is more common in this age group than in the older years.

One of the differences between children and adolescents and adults is that children live according to the pleasure principle of instant gratification while their older counterparts operate on the reality principle of delayed gratification. At some point, though, we adults have to ask ourselves how long we can delay the gratification. If we aren't paying attention to our need for self-respect, belonging, and believing, we can't participate in the pleasures of these years. Our lives inevitably head for a fall if we allow the rat race to continue.

With this said, I'm going to suggest the following to those of you in this age group who are trying to cope with the very significant pressures of this stage of life. First, brace yourself. Turning your life around inevitably involves fear. Then face yourself. Accept responsibility for the part you have played in your problems and accept that all humans have strengths and weaknesses. Pace yourself. Never push yourself beyond what your body and soul tells you is possible for you to do. And finally, give yourself the grace of respect, patience, time. Live according to your own value and belief system and give yourself permission to not "make it" in the knowledge that the pressures shed will be peace gained. What you will achieve will be an inner home for you rather than an empty shell to show to others.

5. All Work and No Intimacy

DURING ONE OF OUR SESSIONS, KAREN BROUGHT in an old photo album to show me. The photographs in the beginning of the album were fairly typical of a middle class North American family with one child. They centered on the achievements of the Gillespies' pretty blonde daughter — Karen performing at piano recitals, Karen receiving writing awards, Karen graduating from high school and college. As she turned the pages, it occurred to me that there was a seriousness about the photographs that in itself was rather sad. Where were the pictures of little friends with goofy grins, or the family dog begging for food, or a simple shot of Karen doing something perfectly ordinary? As we reached the end of the college graduation photos, the album suddenly turned into a scrapbook, full of clippings either written by Karen or about her. Between the two there seemed to be a five-year gap. "I didn't keep any of my wedding photos or any of the pictures we took during our marriage," she explained. "The marriage was a complete and utter failure."

I could imagine the photographs that had been there. The wedding photographs of Chris, the tall, athletic groom, and Karen, his striking bride. The honeymoon trip to Europe. The first apartment decorated in the old pine furniture and bright colors of the early seventies. The first car. As graduates of the same school of journalism, they had been considered the perfect match, particularly by Karen's parents, Bob, a business magazine editor, and Helen, a librarian. Immediately after the honeymoon, the new couple moved to a small university city where Chris had landed a job on the community's only paper. Although the newspaper was not a major daily, it had a solid reputation in publishing circles, and both Chris and Karen were excited at the opportunity it presented Chris. Caught up in the excitement of making a home together and moving to a new city, neither of them thought much about what Karen's life would be like in the months and years to come. Karen was caught in the vise that squeezed women in the seventies: fulfill yourself, yet be a proper wife at the same time.

"I played the role of dutiful young wife to a tee. He was offered a job, so away we went. That was the way I was raised." But Karen had also been raised to be ambitious and successful, and soon the two contradictory roles began to collide. While Chris departed each day for the camaraderie and constant commotion of the newsroom, Karen shopped or cleaned or sat at a desk in their bedroom writing the odd free-lance article. Over the next few years, as Chris was given added responsibility and praise in his job, Karen saw her own skills growing rusty with disuse. Her growing envy of Chris was mixed with her first feelings of failure.

Unfortunately, Chris was too self-absorbed in his own accomplishments and goals to see the effect their new life was having on his wife. He blindly followed the pattern he had witnessed in his parents' traditional marriage — the man at the office and the woman at home. "He could never understand how humiliating it was for me to have to ask him for money. He thought I had an easy life. He couldn't understand what the fuss was about. I couldn't make him see that I didn't want an easy life! I needed a challenge." As his confidence in his writing abilities grew, Chris began to take on the role of teacher with Karen, picking up articles she had written and criticizing them, or writing sarcastic notes on them that she would find in the morning. This hurt and infuriated her, not only because it showed a lack of sensitivity on Chris's part, but also because, as they both knew, she had been the brighter and more talented student in their university days.

It would have been good at this stage in her life for Karen to have been able to talk to someone about her frustration. Her parents, for example, would seem a logical place to turn, but they continued to receive glowing reports from her. This isn't unusual in this type of family. Unintentionally, the Gillespies had always given their daughter the message that they wanted to hear only the good news, not the bad. She had lost touch with her out-of-town school friends, and most young women her age in her new community were either starting a career or raising a family. Because Karen didn't feel comfortable with either group, she found it difficult to make any friends. Chris was little help in this regard. When he wasn't immersed in his work, his own social life revolved around male team sports — baseball in the summer, hockey in the winter. His absences from home became more and more frequent.

At the end of four years, Karen felt left out of Chris's life and unable to make a satisfying life of her own. In an attempt to change what had become a desperately unhappy life for her, she decided that this would be a good time to have a baby. She had always loved children. She would put her career on hold and devote herself to being the perfect mother. Chris, however, had other plans. "He had a thousand reasons for not ever wanting a child, all centering on his needs and goals. It wasn't so much that he didn't want a child. That maybe I could understand. It was his totally self-centered attitude about it and everything in our lives that drove me crazy. I was just along for the ride. He saw no reason to change anything in his life to suit me. Quite frankly, I don't think he ever really loved me, and at the end of the marriage I couldn't understand why I'd married him in the first place. He was just your average insensitive male jock with a superiority complex."

Before their fifth wedding anniversary, Karen left her husband, with few regrets about Chris no longer being in her life. Convinced that her vulnerability during the years of the marriage had its root in being too dependent on another person, she resolved never to get so deeply involved again. Her career was resumed with a vengeance fueled by several years of inactivity and a deep-rooted desire to show Chris how wrong he had been about her. In the next several years, she worked long hours and with tremendous dedication and energy. Her work became her life. By the time she was thirty-five, Karen had outshone her former husband in every way professionally. She wrote a political opinion column for one of the major newspapers and, because she was frequently interviewed or asked to appear on panels, her attractive face was familiar to television viewers across the country. The winner of two journalism awards, she had, in a relatively short time, "made it" by most people's criteria for success.

Heading for a Fall

"And what about your personal life?" I asked.

"I didn't have a personal life," she replied. "I just had a life."

Since the end of her marriage, Karen's professional and personal lives had indeed merged to a great degree. If she had had too much time on her hands in her former life, in this one there was not enough time. Her work occupied about eighty hours of each week. What "spare" time she did have was spent in mainly solitary pursuits — working out at a gym in the newspaper's office building or watching news programs on television in her elegant two-bedroom condominium. The few women friends she had were colleagues, whom she met infrequently for lunch or dinner. Over the years, there had been a few affairs, but she had the impression that her success drove some men away on a personal level. In any event, she was not interested in a committed relationship. Intimacy, for Karen, seemed to cause more trouble than it was worth.

She had witnessed its shortfalls in the marriage of her parents, who had had a verbally combative relationship ever since she could remember. And certainly her own marriage had not given her much cause to believe in the institution. Even the marriages of her friends were not exactly examples of wedded bliss. Although Karen worked well with men on a day-to-day basis, her trust in them had been severely damaged by her one-sided relationship with Chris. Keeping people, particularly men, at arm's length prevented the possibility of exposing her vulnerabilities to another possible attack.

Karen, of course, would never have admitted that she had any vulnerabilities. After leaving Chris, she had concentrated on becoming a strong, successful, independent woman. She rarely complained to anyone and never allowed her emotions to show. Her cool exterior was the coping mechanism that helped her get on with her life and convinced her that she was worthy. A close personal relationship with anyone was equated in her mind with weakness, perhaps even failure. In the greedy eighties, independence and money were valued above all else, and Karen was the epitome of this ideology. Karen's myth about herself was that she needed no one, and that achievement in life meant power, money, and recognition.

By 1983, she had certainly attained all three. She had made the switch from print to television several years previously and, as the co-host of a successful public affairs program, was at the pinnacle of her career. Why, then, as she moved toward the milestone of forty was she increasingly unhappy? Although, again, she wouldn't have admitted it, Karen was lonely. Living alone is no picnic for many adults, and protracted loneliness can be one of the most painful of human emotional experiences. Most of us want a companion with whom to share our hopes, joys, pain, and love. Or we need family or close friends who can fill this supportive role in our lives. Karen had neither.

Another reason for her unhappiness was the lack of satisfaction she derived from her work. Part of the problem was that she could never enjoy her success for its own sake. From early childhood, she had been pushed to try harder and go further. Each achievement was praised but tacked onto the praise was the expectation that she could and, indeed, would accomplish something even more wonderful next month, next year, or whenever. There was a sense that failure was unacceptable and that each accomplishment was just a step in the ladder to perfection. Under these circumstances, the success people like Karen strive for is ultimately for someone else, and because it is for someone else, the pleasure derived from it is muted. As a child, Karen worked hard to gain the approval of her parents. After her divorce, she continued to compete with a man who was no longer there, a man whose approval she had not been able to win. The enjoyment of each success was thus colored by negative, malicious thoughts about Chris. When Karen reached the top of her profession, there was nowhere else to go.

One night, while lying in bed, she finally put away the notebook in her mind that tallied up her successes and infrequent failures and asked herself what Karen Gillespie wanted. "Out of the blue it came to me. What I really wanted was a baby. I couldn't believe the intensity of this thought. It became an almost overwhelming obsession. Oh, it had crossed my mind from time to time before, but this was completely different." It was as if the emptiness of her success made her examine her needs (as opposed to her ambitions) for the first time.

She was almost embarrassed to tell her friends. "Their image of me was of this woman who had liquid steel running in her veins. They were absolutely incredulous that I wanted to have a child." But Karen's friends also sensed that this was a first step — that Karen was also talking about the lack of love in her life and questioning the basic meaning of life. Yes, she needed a nonthreatening relationship; her biological clock was ticking away inexorably; and she thought her depressive feelings would disappear if she had a baby. But beyond that, some inner message from her very soul seemed to be telling her that this was the most meaningful choice she would ever make.

Never one to wait after she had made a decision, Karen made an appointment with her family doctor the following week to discuss the options available to her. Although she was a very fit thirty-eight-year-old, Dr. Segal warned her that there were greater chances of pregnancy and delivery complications and neo-natal birth defects at her age than at a younger age. Not having a husband or lover was also an obvious drawback — procreative sexual intercourse with a relative stranger presented problems of unknown medical history, possible disease, and legal complications. "I briefly imagined asking a husband of a friend to be a 'semen inoculator,' but can you imagine asking someone to do that? Just the phrase itself was so bizarre that I ruled it out almost immediately!" Artificial insemination was another possibility. The semen of an anonymous or "selected" donor could be used to fertilize, in a Petri dish, one of her eggs, which would then be implanted into the lining of her uterus; or spermatozoa could be injected directly into her cervix during ovulation. The final option was adoption, either through conventional channels at home, which involved a long waiting process, or through foreign adoption.

Karen decided to try artificial insemination. She was unprepared, though, for the emotional highs and lows of this method of conceiving. After each insemination, she would believe she was pregnant, only to have her hopes dashed at the onset of her period. She began to feel distinctly unfeminine, as though her failed attempts to conceive were a sign that she was a failure as a woman. "Intellectually, I knew this was nonsense, but emotionally I found it very difficult to deal with." The adoption route began to look more attractive, but as a single woman, she knew the odds were stacked against her arranging an adoption at home, and a foreign adoption presented its own difficulties, among them the lack of assurance that the baby would be healthy.

Riding this emotional roller coaster began to affect every aspect of her life. She was visibly restless and irritable much of the time. At work, her incisive wit was supplanted by a biting abrasiveness. She was losing weight. Her face had a pinched, taut appearance, which makeup couldn't hide. On camera, her flowing commentary had given way to a staccato delivery, punctuated with forced attempts at humor. As she approached her thirty-ninth birthday, her desire to have a baby was turning into an obsession that occupied much of her waking thoughts and many of her dreams.

Still, her viewer ratings remained high, so when Bill Dixon, the news section chief of the network, called her into his office, she had no idea of what was coming. What he coolly told her was that her contract would not be renewed after the season ended in thirty days' time. The show needed a new voice, apparently that of Allison Jones, a woman sixteen years her junior. "Ironically, the old voice literally couldn't speak. Everything seemed to just seize up — my body, my brain, everything." After a few moments of awkward silence, she turned and walked out of the television station and six miles to her apartment. All she remembers is that it took her four hours. The rest of that long walk has disappeared from her memory.

Hitting Rock Bottom

Being fired from a job is a major crisis in anyone's life. If you're a person accustomed to success, and one whose life has revolved around building a career, losing a job can have a particularly devastating emotional impact. In Karen's case, the internal and external supports that enable most people to handle failure were barely existent. Her self-esteem was rooted in her accomplishments at work, and her vaunted independence cut her off from other people. Adding to her despair and humiliation was the public nature of the firing. Newspapers and magazines published a number of articles on her dismissal, the most hurtful being the ones that delighted in the fall of one of the media's success stories. "It was the night of the long knives. I was called arrogant, ruthless, narcissistic, insensitive. They criticized my hair, my clothing, anything seemed to be fair game. It was truly unbelievable. I should never have read all that garbage, but I did. I partly believed it, too." She booked off sick from work and hid in her apartment, with the phone unplugged and the television off.

"I remember standing on my balcony looking out over the valley behind the building. The leaves had turned and I knew that what I was looking at was beautiful, but the awful thing was I didn't have any sense of how beautiful it was. I couldn't touch it. It was as though a veil hung between me and the woods."

Already slipping emotionally from the difficulties in having a baby, Karen's distress increased markedly after her dismissal. The media criticism and exposure, and in fact the firing itself, merely served as the final straw, though. The major cause of her depression was still her failure at bringing a child into her life. She lost more weight. Her appetite became nonexistent. She tried to force-feed herself with milk shakes and desserts, but she was no longer able to keep fatty foods down. She wandered through the rooms of her apartment, unable to settle down in one place. Her sleep went from troubled, to erratic, to fitful, to one to three hours a night at most. In the mornings, she awoke feeling tense and numb at the same time.

For the first time in her life, Karen experienced feelings of intense loneliness. She didn't feel that her parents were available to her, and she had never been dependent on her friends for anything. They recognized this, and in turn didn't turn to her for help in their times of need. They contacted her after her dismissal, but she brushed off their concern with a false lightheartedness. "They had no idea how much I wanted a family of my own or how terrified I was at that point in my life. It wasn't their fault. I hadn't nurtured the relationships, and because I hadn't, I didn't feel that I could all of a sudden start pouring out my guts to them."

When her weight plummeted twenty-five pounds, fear drove Karen back to see Dr. Segal. The doctor found it difficult to hide her shock at Karen's gaunt appearance. The gradual but significant weight loss had been noted by those who saw Karen regularly, but they had attributed it to deliberate dieting. Dr. Segal, on the other hand, hadn't seen her patient in almost a year, and the contrast was dramatic. Karen looked emaciated, so much so that Dr. Segal initially concluded that Karen was suffering from anorexia nervosa, a syndrome in which people, usually women, deliberately starve themselves because of a misconception that they are overweight. However, after talking to her, it became clear that this was a woman with severe psychological problems rather than one with solely an eating disorder.

In her sixties, Dr. Segal was a kindly mother figure to most of her patients. She never felt, though, that she had gotten to know the real Karen Gillespie. There was never enough time. Karen inevitably sandwiched her medical appointments between other more important meetings and dominated the conversation once she was in the doctor's office. Now this tough, accomplished woman looked frail and very needy. Dr. Segal's gentle questioning led to quiet tears and admissions that Karen would never have made a year previously.

She told her doctor about her estrangement from her parents, her long-dissolved marriage, her lack of intimate friends, the absence of a partner in her life, her recent passionate desire for a baby, her inability to conceive, and her unexpected firing. It was a long list, and any one of the problems on it was more than enough to contribute to emotional stress. Taken as a group, they constituted a recipe for internal conflict and despair. When Karen confided that it was difficult to get through each day without considering ending her life, Dr. Segal was naturally concerned about her patient's health and safety. She gave Karen my name, but told her that even if she didn't have all the symptoms of clinical depression, she would still recommend psychotherapy. Dr. Segal was struck, as I was the following week when I met Karen, by the isolated life that this outwardly socially assured, confident woman led. But when she expressed concern that this was an unnatural way for anyone to live, Karen launched into a kind of defense, telling her doctor that she cherished her independence above all else in her life.

"I had very mixed emotions about our talk. It was a relief to share the pain that I was feeling, but it was so upsetting to be told that I needed help because of the way I'd chosen to live. I found that very hard, if not impossible, to accept." Yet when she returned to her apartment, it suddenly felt sterile, removed from humanity. For the first time, she saw it as others must see it. There was nothing of a personal nature to warm it — no photographs of friends or relatives, no silly cartoons taped to the fridge, no mementoes from vacations — just a sophisticated designer-decorated eyrie far removed from the life of the city below. The silence of the rooms was difficult to endure. She sat on the edge of the sofa with her hand on the telephone receiver, desperately needing to connect with someone but unable to bring herself to dial anybody's number.

New Beginnings

It is perhaps unfortunate that so many of us seek a spiritual dimension in our lives only when the chips are down. It may be done with a great deal of thought and planning, or a surprising drift into the spiritual realm may take place. In Karen's case, her inability to confide in friends or family that day drove her, on impulse, to visit the Anglican church not far from her home. This made little sense to her at the time, just as suddenly wanting a baby had seemed so incongruous months before. She had described herself as a lapsed Anglican or as an agnostic for much of her adult life, but during this period of escalating loneliness, she found herself asking God for help.

"It was a different church than the one I had attended as a child, but it looked and smelled and sounded the same — the same light pouring through the stained glass, the smell of the polished wood, even the creaking sound that the kneeling board makes as you pull it down. In those moments when I was praying, I felt like a child again. I felt that God was there, that I wasn't alone and didn't need to be alone. She didn't immediately reply to my prayers," she remembers wryly. "But in a strange sense I did feel like I had spiritually come home. I suppose that sounds clichéed, but I did feel that."

Walking out of the church, Karen felt cleansed, as though she had been purged of something that had been preventing her from moving forward. She then took another surprising step. She responded to an ad in the paper, advising readers that Elizabeth Waters, "The Renowned Psychic," was visiting for "one day only" and would be accepting appointments at a downtown hotel. Karen made an appointment, which she went to with some trepidation and a great deal of embarrassment. "It didn't seem like something a supposedly intelligent person would do, but I was quite amazed at what she told me about myself." In fact, people undergoing turmoil in their lives often do turn to psychics, astrologers, and other non-traditional "helpers" in an attempt to bring some semblance of meaning to their lives. Much depends on whether a person takes comfort in otherworldly experiences and can incorporate them into a larger belief system.

There are all kinds of healers, therapists, and therapeutic techniques. Not every person or problem will respond to identical approaches. Some respond to a "medical model," others to supportive or insight-oriented psychotherapy, and still others to behavior modification approaches. Group or family therapy is also widely used. In a traditional setting, the therapists may be psychiatrists, psychologists, social workers, and various types of counselors.

In addition, alternative therapies are increasingly popular, either in conjunction with more traditional methods or on their own. These include mystical and occult experiences (such as the visit Karen made to the psychic), spiritual healing, encounter groups, EST, Asian meditation and yogic techniques, Gestalt, co-counseling, Twelve-Step, and so on.

I saw Karen later that week. The contrast between the vibrant, beautiful woman I had seen on television and the thin, tremulous woman sitting in my waiting room was as surprising for me as it had been for Dr. Segal. After listening to her story, told haltingly through tears, we talked about how we could work together on her recovery. The week before she had recognized her pattern of avoiding intimacy and dependency, at all costs. Now she was paying the price and didn't want to repeat the same mistakes. This recognition was an important first step, but not without its own drawbacks.

When someone has spent most of her life listening to praise about herself, it's painful to hear that a quality she held dear has in fact been destructive. Karen had experienced this when she had been told by Dr. Segal that her independence was likely at the root of her problems. Our recurrent destructive patterns fit like old shoes for a while. They're familiar and comfortable and may even be associated with pleasure. They initially serve to reduce anxiety or to protect us from the ups and downs of ordinary life. Certainly this is the case in alcohol and substance abuse, anti-social behavior, gambling, and other behaviors that artificially reduce inner pain and fill that sense of emptiness human beings carry to varying extents, at different times, and with different levels of tolerance. Unless these destructive behaviors or patterns are pointed out to us, we tend to repeat them again and again.

At midlife, Karen was ready to welcome people into her life, but it was a frightening process for her. She began by calling her parents. She wanted "to touch their voices" with the telephone call, to reach out to them and feel their love. "I was ready to accept that these people, for all their faults and high expectations over the years, did in fact love me." The Gillespies were delighted to hear from their daughter, who had called only on birthdays or holidays in the past few years. They had stopped calling themselves because she had always seemed too busy or disinterested in their lives. Much to their surprise, she talked to them openly about the changes in her life and asked if she could come home for a long weekend.

Karen's second call was to two of her friends, Lee and Patricia. They were both probably a bit suspicious of Karen's motives in wanting to see them. In the past, she had tended to meet them only when she needed a professional favor. Not knowing that she was afraid to get close to people, they had mistaken her arm's-length distancing for arrogance. At lunch that day, after listening to a Karen they had never met before, they both asked what they could do to help. In the past, such a question would have been interpreted by Karen as an intrusive assault on her independence and competence to run her own life. This time she started to cry. "I can't tell you what it was like to have them both hug me. That's such a natural, simple thing for most people, but not for me."

In addition to nurturing these relationships, Karen also continued to explore her spiritual beliefs in these months of recovery. She began attending different churches on the weekends in search of a spiritual community in which she would feel comfortable. During the week, she met with me and explored what in her life was most meaningful to her as an individual. Children, she discovered, were still very important to her. After volunteering as a Big Sister, it became even more apparent to her how much she wanted to raise a child of her own. Later that year, she began the process of arranging a foreign adoption.

Five Years Later

Karen has resumed her writing career. She writes a weekly syndicated column and occasionally appears on television panels during political crises and elections. She prefers this type of work because it gives her the time to spend with her adopted daughter, Erin, who is now seven months of age. It took a long time to arrange the adoption, but it was obviously time well spent. Karen is a doting, loving mother, and Erin is doing well.

There is no man in Karen's life, but there is intimacy. Her close female friends all act as godmothers to her daughter. She has learned to share her feelings with them, to ask for help, and to be available to them when they are in need. Her parents are part of her life again, although she is determined to protect her daughter from the "you can do better" pressures they placed on her as a child. All these relationships have enriched her life immeasurably.

6. Running Scared

RON BERSANI WAS ARRESTED JUST BEFORE HIS forty-sixth birthday in the law offices of Wilmot, Elkind and Bersani. Two detectives read him his rights and led away the handsome, stylishly dressed lawyer. In the outer working areas of the firm, he was intensely aware of the absence of sound and movement as he passed through them. The secretaries and law clerks sat or stood by their desks, some staring, some looking away in embarrassment. No one talked. The computer keyboards were silent. Sweat had begun to run down his sides and, although his legs felt weak, he had an almost irresistible urge to run. As he left each section, an urgent chattering started up behind him, following him through the reception area and into the elevator, sending him down to a waiting squad car.

One of the top students in his law school class, Ron had risen quickly in his profession. His reputation as an extremely shrewd and eloquent courtroom "performer" and his high number of major courtroom victories were well known; so much so that, once he was hired on a case, the opposing counsel would often try to settle rather than risk a courtroom battle. His clients, who tended to be prominent and wealthy politicians, industrialists, or professionals, paid highly for his services. Among his colleagues, he was feared and respected, rather than liked or disliked. As one of his partners had once told him, in a not altogether complimentary tone, he was "too good to be true."

Ron, however, didn't believe it and kept waiting for the truth to be exposed. He felt that his flamboyance covered his average abilities, that it was only his charm, eloquence, and drive that propelled him to the top. There was a sense that the praise he received was undeserved and his success was unreal in some way.

Despite these vague, uneasy feelings, Ron and his glamorous wife, Sybil, remained on the fast track to success. They had met at a party while Ron was in law school and Sybil was enrolled at a fashion institute; it was, they said, love at first sight. Twenty years later, Ron had succeeded in becoming a partner in a prestigious law firm, and Sybil owned two boutiques. Like many other urban couples on the way up, the Bersanis had extremely full professional and social calendars, which left them little private time together. Their two children, Michael, twelve, and Jenny, ten, were small copies of their parents. They attended private schools, where they worked and played as hard as Mom and Dad. Both were enrolled in numerous after-school activities, which kept them occupied during the week and on the weekends, not always without complaint. When asked to go to a family get-together one Sunday afternoon, Michael had been heard to whine, "But it's my afternoon off!" The affluent, socially prominent Bersanis scarcely had time to breathe.

Once in a while, the head of this spinning top of a family seemed to change into someone else. Normally charming, at times he would become quiet, gloomy, irritable, and demanding. Outsiders never saw this side of him. His family simply put it down to pressures at work and stayed out of his way. Ron, on the other hand, knew that these periods of melancholy had plagued him since adolescence. They reminded him of his mother's frequent bouts of depression, which would send her to bed for days. Although she had been hospitalized a few times over the past thirty years, regular medication seemed lately to have helped. Because of his mother, when Ron experienced one of his own black moods, despair was mixed with apprehension. Was his own moodiness a forerunner of worse things to come?

When his mother wasn't ill, Ron's family had been warm, demonstrative and vocal. His father, Nico, had always been, even in his native Italy, a barber. His mother, Maria, had worked in a bakery when they first arrived in North America, but as her husband had become established, she stayed at home to raise their three sons and a daughter. Ron was the eldest. Even as a child, he understood that as the first-born son, he was expected to succeed.

This pressure on a first-born child to succeed is not unusual in immigrant families. I could empathize with Ron because my own background is very similar. I and most of my friends were children of immigrant parents, and every one of us knew implicitly what we had to do. As the eldest children, we were made to feel a kind of built-in obligation to repay our parents for all they had suffered in leaving their roots to come to a new land. This seems illogical until you realize that most immigrants will say that they have emigrated, not to further their own lives, but to give their children a better start in life. They scrimp and save and work long hours so that their children can go to the best schools. In return, their children, especially the eldest son, is expected to produce.

In Ron's case, his parents' high expectations were coupled with his mother's pushiness. As in Karen's family, nothing Ron achieved was ever quite good enough for his mother, particularly when she was suffering from her illness. When she became agitated, she would often begin to berate him for his inadequacies. Although he was successful at school and sports, he felt a tremendous pressure to do better. Self-doubt was a constant companion. To the outside world, however, Ron appeared to be a relaxed, affable kind of kid. He had learned early in life that people responded to him in a more positive way if he showed competence rather than weakness, but the price of this deception was the dark moods that would paralyze him at times. "I would be doing fine, passing my exams with honors, scoring touchdowns or whatever, and then, bang, this overwhelming sense of fear would come over me. I'd get into bed, pull the covers over my head, and lie there whispering, 'I can't do this any more. I can't do it. I can't do it. I can't do it.' "

Rather than examining what was at the root of his depressive periods, throughout his life Ron either sought shortcuts to pleasure, which gave him temporary relief, or he sought major professional success, which gave him recognition, praise, and money. Even as a child, he had learned that he could improve his mood by risk-taking. Just riding his bike too fast or climbing a tall tree was not enough, though. Ron took small bills and change from the wallets of his parents or his friends' parents and shoplifted from stores. In his teens, stealing served two purposes: it enabled him to own something he couldn't afford, and it was something he could do all by himself, for himself, and get away with it. He discovered that it also gave him a rush and kept his dark moods at bay.

Heading for a Fall

In part, we encourage people to take risks and admire those who put themselves on the line. Business literature is full of examples of men and women who have gone that one step further and seized the brass ring. Usually their risk-taking is legal and morally acceptable. But by the time Ron reached his forties, he had escalated his risk-taking into areas that were neither moral nor legal: He was using cocaine, embezzling from trusts he managed, and having casual sexual affairs with clients. The excitement associated with all three helped minimize the feelings of low self-esteem and despair that he had had trouble coping with all his life. "I knew what I was doing was dead wrong, but I couldn't seem to stop myself. Besides, it all felt so good at the time."

Ron had been introduced to cocaine by some of his high-rolling clients. He experienced a transient high whenever he sniffed a line or two, forgetting his guilt for deceiving Sybil, the pressures of his work, and the fact that he was stealing his clients' money. "I'd convinced myself that I was just borrowing it. I'd plan on putting it back the following week and then that week would come around and I'd need more money to pay off my coke debts or some other debt, so I'd 'borrow' again." After a while, a couple of lines of coke weren't enough. He needed more to achieve the same elevated mood, the same artificial euphoria. Using more would also stave off the inevitable crash that always followed.

I've treated a number of patients with cocaine addictions. It's one of the hardest habits to kick, because cocaine causes a craving unlike any other substance known. Eventually the drug produces only a brief high, followed by fatigue and depression, but by that point the user is addicted. All addicts talk about the void inside themselves that the high they get on drugs fills. It's common after users try to stop, either by themselves or through treatment, for them to forget the negative aspects of the drug and to remember how great it felt at such and such a time. They begin to think about using again. "Maybe this time I can handle it" is a common refrain. This is particularly true if they have been unable to find any kind of peace within while off the drug.

Ron had attempted to give up cocaine a number of times by flushing what he had down the toilet or giving it away. His resolve to quit never lasted very long. He returned to it again and again. Sybil noticed his increasing spells of moodiness, but, as always, gave him the benefit of the doubt. This type of implicit collusion, where those closest to the addict blind themselves to his or her habit, gives the addict a kind of permission to continue. This was certainly true in the Bersani family.

Paradoxically, for a time, all of Ron's self-destructive activities didn't affect his success at work. Although he was on a treadmill he couldn't seem to get off, he was doing exceptionally well professionally, simply because he was an intelligent man who was a master at the cover-up game. At forty-five, though, Ron's world began to slowly unravel.

Financially, the Bersanis were seriously overextended. They had bought a new home a few years previously in one of the city's most exclusive areas, and Sybil's passion for horses had resulted in the purchase of a farm. Expensive entertaining, overseas vacations, private schools and all the other accoutrements of a wealthy life style also began to take their toll on the family's finances. To keep up, Ron was forced to work harder and to illegally borrow more money from his clients' trust accounts. Living on the edge was no longer accomplished with the consummate ease of former years. Ron was now running scared much of the time. "I felt caught up in this incredible web of lies. I seemed to spend half my life lying to people." The stress was beginning to show.

Sybil was the first to notice. For years, she, like Ron, had accepted the fairy-tale perception of their marriage held by outsiders. The pictures in the society pages invariably showed an elegantly dressed, beaming twosome, who were unfailingly polite and seemingly loving toward each other. In private, their marriage was an empty shell. Now, at forty-two, Sybil was beginning to ask herself typical midlife questions about the quality of her own life and particularly her marriage; when she began doing this, the denial mechanisms that had been in place throughout her married life began to crumble. No longer willing to make excuses for Ron, she became increasingly aware of his white lies and inconsistent behavior. "She didn't know what was going on, but she knew something was up. She'd ask me questions I couldn't answer about the money in the accounts or where I'd been this night or that night. This woman I was seeing kept calling the house and hanging up, so she suspected I was having an affair. I kept lying but I didn't fight back when she got mad. I figured I deserved every name in the book."

Knowing that what he was doing was destructive for himself and his family, it seems reasonable to ask why he didn't simply stop. If his marriage was failing, why didn't he arrange to see a marriage counselor with Sybil? If he was having problems coping in a drug-free way with stress or feelings of failure, why didn't he make an appointment with a psychotherapist? And if he was beginning to hate himself because of his dishonest activities, why not just stop them? Unfortunately, it was difficult, if not impossible, for Ron to follow any of these paths. There was a part of him that believed the excitement of money, sex, or coke was an integral part of his life, even though they hadn't worked to alleviate his black moods in a long time. He lived with the unrealistic expectation that perhaps he could regain the control over his life that he had had a few years back. Such thoughts inevitably lead to a life that is lived in the future — "Next week something will come up and everything will be okay" — or in the past — "If only I could get back to where I was, everything would be okay."

Hitting Rock Bottom

The present caught up to Ron in one short month in the spring. Through some amateur sleuthing, Sybil had found some concrete proof of his latest relationship, as well as his drug use. By that time, it scarcely mattered to her. She knew their marriage was in name only and she wanted out. "Sybil moved with the kids to the farm. The kids were really upset, but I had the feeling they weren't too surprised. I hadn't been around very much. We hadn't done anything as a family for a long, long time." Two weeks later he was arrested for embezzlement. Over the past year, a few of his clients had asked questions about the exact disposition of their funds. Ron thought he had given them satisfactory explanations, but two of them had complained to his law partners and an internal investigation had been launched. "I knew I was finished as soon as those two cops showed up at my door. When you're a lawyer, being placed under arrest is the end of the road. All those years of studying and working your way up go down the tube in an instant. At that point, I didn't care. My wife and kids were gone. I was just waiting for the other shoe to fall, and it did."

Out of some sense of loyalty, one of the other partners arranged for Ron to be released from jail on a hefty bail. Not surprisingly, it was made clear to him that this was all he could expect from the firm. Back at home, he had two difficult phone calls to make — one to Sybil and his children and the other to his parents. "Sybil had already heard. The grapevine's pretty good among our friends. She didn't want to talk about it. It was basically 'Talk to my lawyer,' which had a certain poetic justice to it. The kids were more embarrassed than anything else, and my parents of course were devastated." He hung up the phone, feeling a profound sense of loss. Humiliation and powerlessness in a man who had always been seen as a master of any situation was as dramatic a change as one could experience. Ron had come to the end of his rope.

He quickly found the cocaine he had hidden in his closet, but as he pulled it out he realized that a quick fix was not what he needed. In any event, it was unlikely that it would help. The early highs he had experienced when first using, which had brought feelings of omnipotence and well-being, had given way to brief highs followed quickly by depression, anger, and fear. Ron sat on the bed wavering between using the cocaine and tossing it out. He finally decided to flush it down the toilet, because he felt that on the off chance it did make him forget, he didn't deserve to forget or feel better. His actions, he believed, were unforgivable.

As he had done as a teen-ager, Ron curled up under the comforter on the bed, feeling unconnected to the world around him. His thoughts no longer formed in any logical way. They flitted from the past to what awaited him in what had become a very uncertain future and then back again to the past. In his adolescence, there had always been a way out, either through working harder or thrill-seeking. At forty-six, there seemed to be no way out. Suicide was an alternative for Ron, just as it had been for the other people in this book. The previous year, he had bought a revolver in a Florida gun shop. At the time, he had some cocaine debts and was afraid that his suppliers might harm him. Although he didn't know it, this kind of suspiciousness is not unusual for chronic cocaine users and is a prelude to full-blown paranoia. The gun was still in a locked drawer of the desk in his study.

New Beginnings

For the same reason he had rejected using cocaine, Ron decided against suicide. He saw it as another way to run away from his problems. Yet instead of feeling cleansed by this decision, he felt even worse about himself. "I felt I deserved everything that was going to be thrown at me." Looking back over the past several years that night, he saw himself as a fictional character invented by himself. His reputation as a lawyer was built on lies; he had abused the trust of his clients, partners, and family. His reputation as a loving husband and father was also built on lies; he hadn't loved or felt loved by Sybil for years and, although he loved his children, he had spent little time with them. Now that he had been revealed for the sham he was, he was ready to accept his fate.

That evening Ron looked in the "mirror" and confronted himself for the first time. His willingness to accept punishment was a definite step forward, certainly not a pleasant one, but a clear move in the right direction. The decision to stop running away from life and to take responsibility for one's actions is never an easy one to make. Some of us have to hit rock bottom before we can even contemplate how to turn our lives around. In Ron's case, he had to lose his job, family, and freedom before the process of self-discovery and recovery could begin.

While he waited for his trial to begin, Ron struggled with his losses on his own. His parents didn't abandon him, but he found it too emotionally draining to see the pain and disappointment in their faces each time he met with them. His brothers and sister, on the other hand, were only too glad to leave him alone. "I accepted that. I hadn't been there for them when they needed me. I'd been too busy over the years to keep in touch or to help out. I understood their bitterness." He was also shunned by the group of people he and Sybil had socialized with. Most were business acquaintances or friends of Sybil's, so this was not an unusual response on their part. Over the years, he hadn't made any close friends. Friendships, if you could call them that, had been based on what the "friend" could help him with — career moves, clients, access to cocaine. As the phone remained silent after his arrest, this was one more area of his life that Ron mourned.

In those days of waiting, his lawyer was the only person he had much contact with. Despite Ron's objections, the lawyer had devised strategies that would not only allow Ron to avoid punishment but would actually exonerate him. In another time, Ron would have admired, even reveled in the legal trickery dreamed up by a fellow professional. Now it sickened him. It was yet another way to avoid accountability and another way to go further into debt. He fired the lawyer, forgetting for the moment that the system would assign him another one. (His assets were frozen and he had no cash to pay anyone but a legal aid lawyer appointed by the court.)

His new lawyer was a soft-spoken young woman named Julie Noble. At their first meeting, Ron told her about the charges against him, his drug use, why his wife had left him. It all poured out rather incoherently, partly because he had been so isolated over the past few weeks and partly because she seemed willing to listen. "I waited for some signs of disgust or for her to find some way to withdraw from the case. At her age, I wouldn't have touched my case with a ten-foot pole." Instead, Julie told him about a lecture she had heard him give at law school and how much she had admired him. Her attitude was "Everyone makes mistakes. Let's see what we can do."

Sometimes it takes only a few honest words from a kind person to help someone in crisis on the road to recovery. Ron drove home that afternoon feeling a tremendous sense of relief. Until that point, he had accepted responsibility for his actions but had made no plans for the future. When we are unable to get beyond accepting responsibility, we can become stalled in a mire of self-recrimination, which tends to reinforce all the negative views we have of ourselves. Julie's reaction had surprised him. "It was such a simple thing, but it meant so much to me. Her reaction to me — at what had to be the lowest point of my life — was to me as a person, nothing more. The feeling that she seemed to believe in my worth as a person allowed me to see myself in a completely different light." From that point, he was determined not only to face the legal consequences of his actions but also to learn from the mistakes he had made. For a man like Ron, the decision to step out from behind his mask and face the world honestly was an exhilarating one, more exciting than any of the artificial methods he had used in the past to fill the void he had felt inside.

In the following weeks, his determination to change the course of his life was often overshadowed by the sheer weight of his losses and their consequences. He missed his kids. It was summer and Sybil had taken them to her parents for an extended vacation. Telephone conversations with them were brief and awkward at best. He also knew that he would likely be going to prison, and as his trial date approached, he grew increasingly afraid. "I would lie in bed imagining what it would be like lying in a cell. All the bad prison movies I'd ever seen would replay in my head — gang rapes, beatings, the works."

Julie was a much-needed source of support at this time. Ron found that he was becoming increasingly dependent on her. She kept him realistically oriented by not allowing him to indulge either in excessive denial and magical thinking ("This will all go away") or in self-flagellation ("I'm the scum of the earth. I deserve everything I'm going to get"). She also kept him away from cocaine. Realizing that they were becoming fond of each other, she told him that she would stick by him only if he gave up drugs. Powerful motivational, psychological, and social supports are necessary to counterbalance the craving that coke incurs in a regular user. Julie provided that support for Ron. He, in turn, was surprised to find his desire to continue his relationship with Julie could overcome his desire for cocaine. Not surprisingly, his self-control was temporary; his drug problem was not anywhere near solved.

By the end of the summer, Julie had been able to arrange a sentence of six months in a medium-security prison to be followed by an indeterminate stay in a minimum-security group home. Ron began his stay in prison buoyed by Julie's faith in him and his new-found confidence in himself. The effects of both dissipated rather quickly as the numbing boredom and loneliness of prison life set in. Without Julie, he felt himself slipping back into his old skin. There were a number of temptations — power, drugs, money — that the Ron of a year ago would have found difficult to resist, particularly when he was feeling down. He declined the offers, not because Julie told him, "Here you go again," but because he told himself that it wasn't worth it.

At the beginning of the new year, Ron was moved to a group home whose residents had, for the most part, committed white-collar crimes. The home was located in a small town on the outskirts of a large wilderness area. "In my spare time, I took up landscape painting. I'd always enjoyed art as a kid, but I was always steered away from it by my parents. They thought sports or schoolwork were better ways to spend your time. It was good therapy. I'd always been a city boy. The farm was really Sybil's baby. We hired a local farmer to look after it when we weren't around, and I seldom got up there. Painting slowed me down, made me think, made me aware of the world around me." (In some treatment centers, an art therapy program takes advantage of this form of expression to get at deep-seated conflicts.)

Julie came up to visit every weekend, and they were occasionally allowed to picnic in the park. Ron also saw his children every couple of weeks. Both Michael and Jenny had been badly hurt by their parents' separation and father's arrest. At first their attitude toward Ron had been colored by bewilderment and betrayal, but gradually they had begun to respond to his letters and calls. It was obvious to them that their father was trying hard to make amends for not only the separation and jail sentence, but also for the years of benign neglect on his part. Sybil would still have nothing to do with him, so Julie began serving as an intermediary, driving the children to and from the group home on weekends and delivering gifts on birthdays and holidays.

During the week, Ron attended a weekly group therapy session led by a young psychiatrist, Ian Miller. Its purpose was to help the residents come to grips with their losses, their ostracism from society, and the problems they would face in attempting to resume a normal life. Ron looked forward to the sessions. They provided affirmation that he had not been alone in building a life based on self-deception

— many of the men had similar stories to his own — and they also provided hope that he no longer had to lead his life that way.

The hope that is always necessary when we are attempting to turn our lives around is often overshadowed by anxiety, and Ron's case was no exception. His craving for cocaine was bothering him more than he cared to admit to himself or others. "I was afraid to tell Julie because I thought she might leave me if she knew, and I was afraid to tell Dr. Miller because I was afraid my stay at the group home might be extended." In the end, he realized that he was repeating an old pattern — avoiding a problem by denial and lies. He spoke to Dr. Miller, who felt it was imperative for Ron to enter a residential substance-abuse treatment center as soon as he left the group home. He also told him he suspected that Ron had a recurrent unipolar affective disorder, which translated means a repetitive depression based on biological as well as psychological causes. Although Ron didn't know it at the time, this was the same disorder that his mother had. He was placed on a drug called lithium, which evens out mood swings.

It was at the treatment center that I met Ron and heard his story. A treatment center is not always the answer for every addict, but for Ron it provided the help and support he needed at that time. He was involved in daily group sessions as well as individual work with a counselor. Both gave him further affirmation of his self-worth. There was not one instance among the more than fifty patients whom he met in which the substance abuse had occurred in a vacuum; inner problems had usually predated the drug abuse. It was these often deep-rooted negative feelings that they all worked on. At the end of the ten-week program, Ron left the center with a firm grasp on who he was and the type of person he wanted to be in the future.

Five Years Later

Five years later, Ron is happily married to Julie. "Julie taught me how to love, how to open up to people. I've always been good with people but I never trusted that. I always felt that I was charming them out of their pants. I used to feel negative about other people and myself. Now I'm much more relaxed." They live with their one-year-old child in the country. Julie practices law in a small city nearby, while Ron has returned to college to get his degree in hotel administration. Although his license to practice law is up for reinstatement this year, he is not going to bother to apply.

He has been successful in staying off drugs, attending monthly evening group sessions and lectures at the treatment center. He still takes lithium, but is not seeing a psychotherapist. Ron's treatment program is not based on the AA Twelve-Step model (see Chapter 8), but resembles it in the basic process of first facing oneself, then admitting responsibility and accountability, and, finally, attempting to turn one's life around with the encouragement of the group. Most treatment centers use the group and a strong value system to help individuals move toward a new, more honest life. This is entirely congruent with my understanding that it is through belief (values, ideology, spirituality) and belonging (group participation and acceptance, shared experiences and goals) that a destitute person will return to self-acceptance and fulfillment.

7. Facing Childhood Abuse

WHEN SHE WAS FIVE, JUDY WILSON WAS GIVEN A blue pajama dog, a stuffed toy with a zippered pouch for pajamas that was popular in the sixties. She named her floppy-eared dog Blueberry and wondered afterward if perhaps she should have given it a more fierce name. Each night, she would carefully place the dog on her bed between her and the bedroom door. And sometimes the door would stay shut and sometimes it wouldn't.

At thirty-four, Judy had a daughter of her own and what appeared to be a charmed life. Although their lives had taken different paths, Judy, like Karen, had been envied by many people — Judy for her pampered existence as a young socialite, Karen for her exciting career. Like Karen, Judy was an attractive woman — dark-haired with fine features and eyes that were such a dark brown the pupils seemed to disappear altogether. She shared Karen's aloofness, which in her case most people attributed to a privileged upbringing. Her father, David, was a prominent judge, and her mother, Phyllis, was an heiress whose volunteer work had left little time for Judy or her older brother Jim when they were growing up. They had both gone to private schools as day students. Jim, a naturally gregarious boy, had immersed himself in clubs and sports activities, while Judy remained a loner throughout her school days and beyond.

There is a misconception that loners are always considered to be losers by their peers. In reality, the other girls at Judy's school simply thought she was a first-rate snob, who probably had more deserving friends outside school. Although her classmates thought she was "too good" to associate with them, in reality Judy didn't feel that she was "good enough." We often think we know what people are feeling when they look a certain way, and nine times out of ten we are wrong. In Judy's case, no one could see the shy, frightened girl behind the calm, self-possessed exterior.

After graduation, Judy started work in a well-known downtown law office, where her father had once been a partner. Her marks had been too low for admittance to university, and even if they had been acceptable, she had little ambition. She continued to live at home, dating sporadically, not because she wanted to but because she felt it was expected of her. Until she met Michael Clark, she wasn't interested in becoming intimate with anyone, and she formed a relationship with him less out of love than passive resignation. He seemed honest and reliable. At the age of twenty, she married him. "It seems a very cruel thing to say now, but Michael was in some ways my ticket out of my parents' home."

The red-haired, baby-faced Michael was a Harvard Business School grad, who didn't look old enough to hold the high-paying position he acquired as soon as he graduated from university. His own childhood had been spent in the protected upper-middle-class comfort provided by an engineer father and a stay-at-home mother. It was a quiet home, devoid of openly expressed feelings. Consequently, warmth and empathy weren't a natural part of this young man's personality. Paradoxically, however, this is what had attracted Judy to him in the first place. She had always disliked charismatic, effusive men — men like her father.

When Bonnie was born, Judy felt that at last she had a reason for being. She worked very hard at caring for her daughter and resolved to protect her from any kind of harm. Although she knew that she tended to be overprotective, this was one area of her life in which she took great pride. At midlife, the Clarks lived in a large Georgian house in an expensive neighborhood. Like her mother, Judy spent much of her time on volunteer committees or entertaining Michael's business clients. Unlike her mother, she had cut back on many of her activities after Bonnie was born so that she could devote more time to raising her daughter. "I was determined to be there for my daughter. I wanted her to know that she came first in my life, that she wasn't somewhere way down on a list."

As Bonnie approached school age, Judy began standing by the side of her daughter's bed each night watching her sleep. The warm feelings that all parents have at such times would be drowned by childhood memories. "I think it was the way she hugged her animals that tore me apart. My stuffed toys were the only witnesses to the horror my father put me through. I'd hug them and hug them and give them all sorts of magical qualities that would keep me safe, which of course didn't work. So when I looked at Bonnie with her little 'friends,' I relived it all again — things I'd tried to put out of my mind for years."

Judy had been sexually molested by her father hundreds of times over a seven-year period from the ages of six to thirteen.

Heading for a Fall

Some incest victims bury the incidents of abuse in their subconscious. This psychological trick protects them from having to face the fact that a parent they love is capable of such acts. The sexual abuse is so difficult to comprehend that it becomes walled off in the mind and separate from memory. After this happens, what remains for the victims is the sense that there is something terribly wrong with them. The reason for this is the difficulty children have in believing their parents are monsters; instead, they believe they are to blame, that they are the "bad ones." Their sense of low self-worth may negatively affect every aspect of their adult lives, particularly their relationships with the opposite sex, and it may only be in counseling that they discover the shattering reason for their personal problems.

Judy, on the other hand, remembered everything. "My father would come late at night after my mother had gone to sleep. He would reek of whiskey. The smell of it would be everywhere. He'd try to make a game of it, saying he'd found his little girl and then he'd proceed to 'find' all the parts of my body. When he was through, he'd always tell me not to tell anyone and I'd always agree." Once she had tried to tell her mother, but her mother, possibly out of fear and an inability to believe the worst of her husband, had refused to listen to her daughter's "stories." Unfortunately, this is more the rule than the exception. I know of countless examples of young girls being criticized, condemned, ostracized, and even ejected from the family for attempting to blow the whistle on an abusive father. The mother often knowingly or unwittingly colludes in perpetuating the abuse.

After suffering the pain of not being believed by her own mother, Judy trusted no one and consequently told no one else of the humiliation and fear she endured at the hands of the eminent Judge Wilson. In the end, as an adult, she and her parents had an unspoken agreement to bury this sordid part of their past. They all pretended it had never happened.

A love-hate relationship with the molester and a deep sense of shame and self-loathing often result from the convoluted emotions of the victim of childhood sexual abuse. It is as if such an incomprehensible experience — the ultimate betrayal — must be the child's own fault. The child cannot believe that her father would do something so heinous, so she develops a curiously passive relationship with her molester and even allows him to do her favors, as when Judge Wilson found Judy her first job.

Judy had continued to see her mother and father after her marriage, "for appearance's sake." Her relationships with both parents were obviously strained. She loathed and feared her father and felt estranged from her mother. Mixed with these negative feelings were the remnants of a child's love for her parents and sadness that she had been denied a loving childhood. After Bonnie was born, she thought it would be good for her daughter to see the grandparents, although she was careful never to leave Bonnie alone with her father. Inwardly, she was also attempting to fight her antipathy toward her parents by putting herself on the line. This is called counterphobic behavior — an individual will overcompensate for his or her fear by repetitively confronting what it is he or she fears.

At thirty-four, however, Judy was finding it more and more difficult to pretend that her world was perfect. She had spent much of her life protecting her father and making sure that no one discovered her secret. Now she was finding that keeping up the facade was taking too much effort. She was feeling increasingly on edge. While Bonnie was napping in the afternoon, she would drink wine in the family room and leaf through magazines, watch soap operas on television, or simply stare out the window. She would feel temporarily soothed, and then the inner torment would begin again. "I was finding it hard to concentrate on planning even the simplest things. I couldn't seem to make any decisions at all. It became quite absurd. I'd stand in front of Bonnie's closet and take the longest time just figuring out what to dress her in." Gradually, she lost all interest in the volunteer and social activities that had been a part of her daily life, became irritable with Michael when he inquired about them, and slept fitfully after the day was through.

"I had these horrible nightmares. Bizarre dreams where my mother would be cutting out my tongue or I would be running through room after room." Possible interpretations of these dreams, which Judy herself came up with, are, for the first: "So that I couldn't tell anyone about my father." And for the second: "So that nobody would catch me and hurt me." Quite simply, Judy's past had caught up with her, and this time it wouldn't leave her alone.

Dreaming is an integral part of the sleep cycle and occurs during the REM (rapid eye movement) period, which accounts for upwards of 20 percent of the sleep cycle. During periods of stress, dreams tend to be more vivid and are sometimes bizarre and frightening. The interpretation of dreams has fascinated people since ancient times. Often, specific and universal meanings are associated with symbols that appear in dreams. More simply, you can interpret dreams by examining your mood and thoughts in relation to the dream to try to determine what your unconscious is telling you.

As happens with many people in crisis, Judy felt trapped in her own private hell. Dreadful secrets destroy any hope of ever finding an inner home unless they are brought into the open and confronted and dealt with. Judy, like many incest victims, didn't know where to turn. Her mistrust of people had prevented her from forming deep friendships, and Michael was not the kind of man who was easy to confide in. "I couldn't imagine telling him about my father — he admired him — and I think I was afraid he wouldn't believe me anyway." She also couldn't bring herself to tell him about two of the results of the incest — her disgust whenever they made love and her self-hatred. It's hard to confess to anyone, let alone your husband, that your life has been based on lies.

Judy's parents, now in their sixties, couldn't understand why she no longer visited them with Bonnie. On the phone, she was brusque with her mother and tried to avoid speaking with her father. When they invited her to visit, she turned them down with a terse "I'm tired" or "Bonnie's so demanding" or "We're busy." Although they both sensed that she was angry at them, she denied that they played any part in her not being able to visit. The confusing signals that Judy was giving them reflected her own confusion and are classic signs of an approach-avoidance conflict, in which we want and don't want something with equal intensity.

What Judy badly wanted was to confront her father with the suffering he had caused her. Actually doing it was another story. In her nightmares and daydreams, she saw him angrily denying everything, her mother nodding her head at every bitter word he flung at her. The next instant she would be standing in a courtroom. The door to the judge's chambers would open and her father would walk slowly to the bench. Far above her, he would glare down and pronounce her mentally unfit to be a mother. As Michael and Bonnie looked on, she would be led away, screaming.

Hitting Rock Bottom

When we are no longer able to sustain our myths about ourselves, when the mask slips, it's often easier to hide from the world. Judy hid inside her house. She stayed there because it had gradually become unbearable to leave. Over the past four months, as her inner agony over her lost childhood and inability to confront her father had increased, she experienced moments of heart-pounding terror whenever she walked through the front door. These brief bouts of fear had lengthened in duration, bringing on a condition as close to panic as she had ever experienced. This fear of the outdoors, a condition called agoraphobia, had progressed to the point where she was, for all intents and purposes, a recluse. "Sometimes the house felt like a jail. The mini-blinds on the windows began to look like bars. I spent one mad couple of minutes one day racing all over the house pulling up the blinds because I couldn't stand looking through them any more, but I still couldn't bear the thought of going outside."

Like Karen, Judy's physical health also began to deteriorate. She lost a significant amount of weight. Her sleep was now limited to three or four hours a night. She would wake up at 3 a.m. and, unable to fall back to sleep, would wait until she heard Bonnie talking to her dolls in the next room before getting up to face another emotionally and physically exhausting day. She was becoming irritable with her daughter now as well as her husband, who finally had to acknowledge that his wife was not going to snap out of whatever funk she was in. It was becoming increasingly obvious that she was unable to cope. Michael found himself helping more with Bonnie but unable to assist his wife in other ways. His inquiries and offers of help were all rebuffed, often in a hostile manner that seemed completely out of character.

It is not unusual for women who have been brutalized by their fathers to contemplate suicide. The shame of the acts themselves, the powerlessness to prevent them, and the despair at the betrayal they represent are heavy burdens to carry. What saved Judy from ending her life was her growing rage toward her father. Her mind was full of seemingly unsolvable questions. "I'd ask myself, 'How could he have done it? How could I have allowed it? Why hadn't my mother protected me?' " Around and around she'd go, seeking answers that never appeared and feeling alternately dead inside or full of anger.

When our anger is dammed up inside, unable to be directed toward its cause, it will often spill over onto the people around us. Judy became more and more abusive toward Michael, particularly after she had been drinking. After one particularly violent outburst, Michael became sufficiently worried about his wife's mental state to call her parents. When he went to see them, his mother-in-law was visibly annoyed at him for having waited so long to tell them about Judy's problems. Curiously, Judy's father seemed unperturbed and reluctant to take any action at all. Michael came away feeling that the old judge didn't want his reputation tarnished by an emotionally disturbed daughter. Since her parents couldn't seem to agree on whether their daughter should be hospitalized, Michael decided to call Iris Dunning, the family doctor.

After meeting with Judy, Dr. Dunning agreed with Michael that his wife needed to be hospitalized before she further harmed herself or others. Judy wouldn't agree to it. "It was my worst nightmare come true — being separated from my child." Because she wouldn't voluntarily admit herself, a certification order was signed by Dr. Dunning, and Judy was admitted to the Psychiatric Unit of a large teaching hospital. (Involuntary hospitalization can be accomplished only if the individual threatens his or her own life, if the individual threatens the life of someone else, or if the life of the individual is in imminent and serious danger. Clearly, Judy was hospitalized on the third ground.) In the car on the way to the hospital, she slouched down in the back seat and refused to say a word to Michael or her mother. She felt powerless and humiliated, yet in a way relieved that perhaps with this step she could "stop dying."

At the beginning of Judy's stay in the hospital, she was visited by a resident in Psychiatry, who was unable to coax much out of her at all. "He was so young. How could he have begun to understand what I had been through?" The nursing staff was kind, but she found that she couldn't open up to them either. It was the patient group that helped her the most. All the patients on the ward were expected to attend group therapy sessions, which were led by a female nurse and a male social worker. There were thirteen patients in the group, of whom six were women. Four of the women had been sexually abused as children by someone they knew well. In the group, they openly spoke about the experience of being abused children and how it had affected their lives. As their anger and despondency poured out, Judy was deeply moved. Although she couldn't bring herself to say anything about her own broken childhood, for the first time in her life she felt a kinship with other people. Just knowing that she wasn't alone and that other abused women felt the same way she did changed her own outlook immeasurably.

The certification order was lifted after seventy-two hours, and Judy left the hospital seven days later. She had missed Bonnie, and while the doctors advised her to remain, there were no legal grounds to keep her in hospital against her will. She went home knowing that she needed to confide in someone before she could begin to get well.

New Beginnings

The next day she called Dr. Dunning, who was pleased to hear that Judy wanted help. She offered to make an appointment for Judy with a psychotherapist, but Judy felt comfortable with her longtime family doctor and was adamant that she didn't want to talk about her problems with a stranger. Reluctantly, Dr. Dunning agreed.

At their first session, Judy told the doctor about the sexual abuse she had suffered as a child. Dr. Dunning, despite all she had heard in fifteen years of practice, was stunned. She had obviously heard such horror stories before; however, this time she knew the victim and the abuser. Although Judy noticed that her doctor was visibly shaken, it was difficult to hold back after all the years of denial and the past few months of rage. "I can't tell you what a relief it was just to talk about it for the first time."

It was clear to both of them at the end of the session, though, that a one-hour outpouring of emotions was not going to undo years of damage. Talking is vital for those whose lives have been torn apart, but it is only a beginning. Dr. Dunning was more than willing to work with Judy, but she knew her patient needed help in other ways too. On my recommendation, she placed Judy on an anti-depressant medication that had been shown to be effective not only in counteracting depression but also in diminishing the panic attacks associated with agoraphobia. Combining psychotherapy with medication is not at all unusual. Although there are often clear historic and current reasons contributing to a depression, anti-depressants can biologically expedite the lifting of one's mood.

Judy refused to see me or any other mental health professional, and, in fact, I thought she was doing just fine with her own doctor. What she did agree to was to attend an incest survivors' group. A self-help group offers its members true empathy. The members understand one another and convey that sense of understanding, because they have all undergone the same trauma in their lives. Judy's brief encounter with group psychotherapy in the hospital had convinced her of its worth, but she was still nervous about revealing her own experiences to strangers. She went to her first meeting in a local community center with a great deal of trepidation. Just getting there was an ordeal. "The pills helped, but I was still deathly afraid of being outside the house, particularly at night. I really had to psych myself up for it."

The women Judy met that night were from all walks of life. They were all dealing with the effects of childhoods that had been destroyed by a man they had trusted. One common theme was the love-hate relationship they had with men. The group leader, who was a counselor from one of the downtown centers for abused women, encouraged them to express their rage, but she also asked them to look at how their behavior affected others and helped them to explore their feelings when they acted in self-destructive ways. She was particularly good at drawing out shy women like Judy.

People sometimes worry that they will be confronted in a group and have their vulnerabilities exposed. Nothing could be further from the truth. Self-help groups are invariably empathetic and nurturing. In talking about the similarities in their lives and their feelings of inadequacy, participants learn that they are not unique. They learn from others how to handle problems and themselves give help as they progress along the path of recovery. One of the most important lessons they learn is self-respect.

Judy left the meeting that night feeling better about herself than she had in a long time, if ever. She had finally taken a constructive step toward ending the playacting that had characterized her life. At the end of a month, with the help of her group, her bi-weekly sessions with Dr. Dunning, and her medication, she began to join the world again. Her panic attacks had subsided dramatically, with the result that she was able to go out on errands or walks to the playground with Bonnie. What she wasn't able to do was to go out socially with Michael. "I hated all men at that point. I had just begun to trust the women in my group. It was too early to trust him. For the first time in my life I was being honest about my feelings, and that's the way I felt. I didn't want to go anywhere with him. I didn't want to have anything to do with him."

At this stage, Judy's relationship with her daughter was the only relationship with a member of her family that was improving. In the past, she had been unable to be spontaneous with Bonnie. Now she was openly affectionate with her. The rest of the family, on the other hand, was kept at arm's length. Her brother lived in another country and was rarely in touch. She never saw her parents. Her mother called occasionally, but was extremely uncomfortable talking to her, possibly because she had guessed the reason for Judy's breakdown. Her father no longer tried to communicate with her at all. And Michael coped with his problems at home by staying late at the office to work. It was a situation that couldn't continue. "I had to come to grips with my relationship with my father and Michael."

She began by talking about her marriage at a support group meeting. "It was easier to begin with Michael than my father." Some of the members were convinced that she should leave Michael. Others thought she should talk to her husband about her past so that he could at least begin to understand her pain and estrangement from her parents and him. If nothing else, it would be a test of his sensitivity. In working with Dr. Dunning, however, she began to realize that not all of the problems in the marriage stemmed from her childhood experiences. The communication between the two of them had been poor, as much due to Michael's cool demeanor as hers. The doctor recommended they see a marital counselor to find out if their marriage could be saved. Ordinarily, three kinds of therapy in a week is more than enough for anyone. In addition to the time, expense, and energy involved, contradictory messages or tasks can often lead to confusion. Because of this, Dr. Dunning suggested that the sessions with her be cut back to once a month so that Judy could continue with her group therapy and see a marital counselor as well.

That evening after Bonnie was in bed, Judy decided to broach the subject of going to counseling with Michael. She found him in the family room where he was stretched out on the sofa reading and sat down across from him. He didn't look up from his book. There probably seemed to be little point. In the past few months, any attempt he had made at conversation had been rebuffed. "I wasn't sure how he'd react to the idea of marriage counseling. He's so conservative, so private. I thought he'd say counseling was okay for me, but not for him." In fact, Michael was more surprised that she had spoken to him than by her suggestion. "He told me that if I hadn't suggested it, he would have, because he was tired of living with someone who obviously didn't want to live with him any more." When Michael told her that he was also tired of being kept in the dark about what was wrong, Judy broke down and told him about her father's abuse. It is always hard to comprehend cruelty inflicted on children, even more so when the abused child is someone you love. "I watched every emotion cross his face — horror, anger, sadness, love. It was the first time I'd ever seen him cry."

The next day they made an appointment with the marriage counselor recommended by Dr. Dunning. In their sessions, the counselor was particularly skilled at getting them to express their emotions. There was anger and resentment on both sides. Judy felt that Michael's work had become more important than his family. Michael was aghast that Judy had equated him with her father and in doing so had essentially abandoned him years ago. After a number of sessions, where they explored their marriage at various stages of their lives, what it meant to each of them, and what they would like to change in it, they both found they wanted it to work, not just for Bonnie's sake, but for their own as well.

For Judy, the work she and Michael did in marriage counseling was another part of the healing process. As she listened to her husband talk about his feelings, she realized that although he wasn't a demonstrative man, he was very loving in his own way. He had stood by her and offered to help countless times over the past months. He had made no demands on her. The main reason she had disliked him so much was because, in her mind, he represented all men. Now she finally saw how truly different he was from her father. "I started feeling so much better about us and our future together with Bonnie."

Judy had come a long way in therapy. She now felt strong enough to begin discussing how she would confront her father. Not all victims of sexual abuse are able to face their abuser. It can be frightening to confront the man who has held so much control over their lives and upsetting if the accusations are denied by the abuser himself or other family members. Judy, however, was determined to stop protecting her father. "He didn't deserve to be protected for what he did to me. He stole something from me and I wanted him to know it. I wanted to be heard." After many weeks of working with Dr. Dunning and discussing the issue with her group, she decided upon a course of action. She would report her father to the police unless he admitted to the abuse and agreed to get help.

With Michael at her side, Judy called her father one evening. It took a great deal of courage. Her hands and voice shook as she asked him to meet her at Dr. Dunning's office later in the week. Although he seemed delighted to hear from her, Judge Wilson asked the purpose of the meeting. "I told him I had some problems that Iris had been helping me with and that I wanted to discuss them with him." After hesitating for a moment, he agreed.

On the day of their meeting, Judy arrived at the office first. Dr. Dunning had cleared her appointments for the rest of the day and they talked for a while before Judge Wilson appeared. He opened the door slowly, appearing tense and much older than she remembered. Judy had written down what she wanted to say in case she felt too intimidated to talk openly. Once they were alone in Dr. Dunning's office, though, she found that she didn't need to use her notes. All the years of pent-up hurt and anger were suddenly released in a rush of angry words. In that half hour of rage, Judy took back control over her life, transferring the shame that she had felt to where it properly belonged — with her father.

Unable to look into his daughter's eyes, Judge Wilson stared at his hands while he asked her what she wanted him to do. Before she had a chance to respond, he began to cry, asking repeatedly for her forgiveness. (Unlike Judge Wilson, many abusers don't apologize for their destructive behavior, but continue to deny that it ever happened.) "I told him that he had to get help. I wasn't prepared to forgive him, but I did say that I still loved him even though he sickened me." That said, she walked out of the office, leaving her father to talk to Dr. Dunning.

Five Years Later

Five years later, Judy lives with Michael, Bonnie, and new son, Eric, in another city. She is going to college, part-time, studying to be a social worker. Michael works fewer hours these days and is more warm and open with his family. Through counseling, hard work, and commitment, their marriage seems to be working. Both of Judy's parents sought help after Judy's confrontation with Judge Wilson. Although their relationship with their daughter is still strained, they do continue to see Bonnie from time to time. No one is playacting any longer.

8. Alcohol Abuse

ALCOHOL HAD BEEN A FOURTH MEMBER OF Henry Williams's family for as long as he could remember. As a small boy, he knew its characteristics intimately — the look of it as it shimmered in a bottle, the sound of it being poured out into a glass, the smell of it on his father's and mother's breath. He resented the money they spent on it, the pleasure and pain they derived from it, and the attention it stole from him.

The Williamses lived in a second-floor flat above a small grocery store. George Williams, a big-boned Irishman, was a would-be novelist who eked out a living writing handbills and the odd radio script, while his wife, Evelyn, tried to maintain her English airs in the "colonies." They had little in common except drinking. Like his own father, George was a hard drinker and often launched into sometimes violent tirades when he was on a binge. "Lady Evelyn," as her friends called her, also drank to excess but was much less open about it; in fact, she frequently chastised her husband for being a drunk and a financial and literary failure. For his part, George railed against her lack of understanding and the incompetence of publishers for turning down his fiction with some regularity. His parents' bickering, fueled by liquor and their bitterness at the hand life had dealt them, was at the center of Henry's earliest memories.

"Although they fought a lot and I was somewhat neglected as a child, I don't think I was unloved. I knew they loved each other and me in their own strange way." To compete with the alcohol and to gain his parents' approval, Henry worked exceptionally hard at school and had the marks to prove it. He also excelled at sports and in music. As he grew older, both parents turned to him for their salvation. Evelyn expected him to transport her to a life of ease and gentility, and George wanted his son to write the great novel that he himself had been prevented from publishing, supposedly due to the ineptitude of the publishers who had rejected his work. Shortly after Henry graduated from college with a degree in English Literature, his father died of cirrhosis of the liver. At his funeral, Henry vowed to write the novel George had never written and to dedicate it to his father.

Twenty-two years later, Henry's dream was still to write something his "old Dad" would admire. In appearance, he resembled George, although unlike his father he had kept his large frame trim through exercise. The curly head of dark hair, the pale skin, and the greenish eyes, he shared with his father. His long fingers and thin lips were the only clues that he was his mother's son. All in all, people who met him in his role as an advertising executive at a large agency considered him a stylish, erudite, witty sort of man. At forty-five, Henry had come a long way from the second-floor walk-up flat of his childhood.

Like Ron Bersani, Henry was admired by his superiors, colleagues, and clients. He had won more than his share of industry awards for the advertising campaigns and slogans he had written and, in return, was paid handsomely for his work. The money allowed him to indulge in a number of activities — sculpture, tennis, sailing, jazz — which helped maintain his image of himself as a Renaissance man. It had also provided him with a recently built cedar and glass house, designed to his specifications and set into a wooded hill on the outskirts of the city. He shared it with his second wife, Meg, a quiet woman with strong angular features, who taught high-school English at a local school.

The couple had no children, although Meg, who was ten years his junior, had been hinting that after nine years of marriage, she was ready for a child. Henry, on the other hand, already had a teen-age daughter, Jennifer, who lived with his first wife, Elizabeth, in another city. Elizabeth had fallen in love with one of his close friends and had left him. After their divorce, she had remarried and moved away. It had been a particularly painful time. Trying to keep up a long-distance relationship with Jennifer had largely met with failure, and he now seldom saw her. He found it difficult to imagine beginning all over again with a new baby at his age.

Every afternoon, before his long commute home by train, Henry would visit his favorite watering hole, an up-scale bar that catered to people in the media. There were always a friendly welcome and a group of fellow writers or would-be writers, who would dissect the latest best seller or controversial magazine piece over a number of rounds. The amount of time he spent there and, on weekends, at a local pub not far from their home had increased markedly over the past few years and had been quietly remarked upon by Meg. She pleaded with him to stop drinking and spend more time with her. He chose to ignore her remarks. Although he had typed out only a few ideas for his novel, he liked to give the impression to his drinking friends that "it was in the works." "'A man needs his friends,' I would say to my wife." He also needed his liquor.

Heading for a Fall

Henry knew he was drinking too much, but he had conveniently convinced himself that this was a trait of all great writers. "I had a list of writers from Dylan Thomas to Faulkner and Fitzgerald to justify it. Pathetic, but true." His mother, who lived in a retirement home, often warned him about his drinking on her visits to her son's and daughter-in-law's home. He ignored her warnings as well as Meg's in the belief that he could stop when he chose to, and at this particular time in his life, he didn't choose to quit. Unlike his father and grandfather, he was an intelligent, successful man and believed that intelligent, successful men did not become alcoholics, particularly at the relatively young age of forty-five.

After five years of this work, drink, and sleep ritual, though, Henry began to admit to himself that all was not perhaps going as well as he had hoped it would at forty. For one, all the varied pursuits he had enjoyed outside the office seemed to be disappearing from his life. He had given up his athletic activities, which had resulted in the beginning of a middle-aged spread, and he hadn't sculpted or attended a jazz session in years. He was, in addition to drinking heavily, smoking over a pack of cigarettes a day. Like many other smokers, he used the fact that he didn't inhale as a way to justify his smoking. It was another lie in a long series of lies to himself and others that helped him avoid his problems. Now he was realizing that his world was shrinking, and that by surrounding himself with fellow drinkers each night and on the weekends, he was, in effect, avoiding the boredom he felt in his marriage and work, the dissatisfaction he felt within himself, and, of course, the writing of the novel.

For all his growing insights into his behavior, Henry continued on his self-destructive path. He was spending less and less time at work. After a few hours at the agency in the morning, he would leave for a "working lunch" and then make his way to the bar. The owners of the agency respected his creativity and probably in a mild way even encouraged his behavior, in the belief that the alcohol went along with his artistic and literary temperament. Eventually, though, matters got out of hand.

One night, after five hours of heavy drinking, Henry fell down a flight of stairs. He was taken to a nearby hospital, where a bad cut to his face was stitched. His wife was called and asked to come and take him home. While he was waiting for her, one of the Emergency Room doctors sat down beside him and told him that if he didn't stop drinking, worse things were going to happen to him than a cut face and blood-stained clothes. His blood alcohol level was four times the "acceptable" level for driving. "I remember protesting that I wasn't driving. I wasn't really listening to what he was saying." Meg, looking drawn and worried, finally arrived and they drove home in silence.

The following week the doctor's predictions came true. Henry's work was no longer up to his former standards. Months earlier, he had begun to assign some of his own writing to two of his junior writers and then passed off their work as his own. Understandably annoyed, one junior had complained to the president of the agency, and Henry had been called on the carpet. It was suggested that he get some professional help for his drinking problem before it affected his work further than it already had. Henry's reaction was to stomp out of the office and head for the bar, where after an afternoon of drinking, he got into a fist fight with a drinking buddy and was asked to leave. After missing his train that morning, he had driven into the city. Now, enraged by the events of the day, he got into his car and sped out of the parking lot. Not noticing that the pavement was wet after a spring shower, he skidded out of control into a line of parked cars. When the police arrived, they found him slouched over the wheel of the car, badly bruised, with one tooth chipped where he had hit the steering wheel, and obviously drunk. For the second time that month, Meg picked him up at the hospital. He had been arrested and charged with drunk driving.

Later that evening, while Henry was watching the news on television, Meg walked into the room and told him that she was leaving him. Rather than being angry, she appeared resigned and sad. "She told me that she wasn't going to sacrifice her own life and health for me any more. She was tired of blaming herself for my drinking and tired of rescuing me." Before Henry had had a chance to collect his thoughts, Meg had left the house. The second blow came the next day when the agency president told him he was no longer welcome at work unless he quit drinking, which he seemed incapable of doing. Nor, at this stage, did he have any intention of stopping. All he could feel was anger at his boss, who seemed heartless to Henry. Facing drunk-driving charges, and with no wife and no job, Henry did what he always did — he went to his favorite bar and got drunk.

Hitting Rock Bottom

In the following weeks, Henry's mood alternated between anger and self-pity. He was angry at Meg for leaving him. Although she had every reason to leave, had left quietly without a scene, and had asked for nothing since her departure, he blamed her for ending their marriage without discussing it with him first. He was angry at the ad agency for firing him. He ignored his unprofessional behavior and poor track record of the past few years and concentrated on his past glories. "I had made a lot of money for them over the years, and I guess my ego wouldn't let me blame myself for the firing. I blamed them." And, lastly, like his father, he was angry because no one recognized his true talents as a writer. The few stories he had managed to write had been rejected for publication. He consoled himself alone in his house with the thought that as soon as this run of bad luck was over, he would show them all how talented he really was.

The only bright spot in his life was the companionship he still found at his downtown bar. While his old friends had dropped away one by one over the years as he had turned from a witty companion into a sarcastic drunk, he could still count on the "understanding" of his drinking buddies at the bar. This was why he was particularly incensed when one of them, after hearing of his problems, took him aside one night and recommended Alcoholics Anonymous. To prove that he wasn't an alcoholic, he decided to show the fellow that he could drink him under the table and still stay sober.

Needless to say, Henry didn't succeed. He passed out in the bar and the police were called when the bartender couldn't revive him. Two policemen took him to the same hospital he had been admitted to before, where he was not exactly welcomed with open arms. Emergency doctors and nurses often tend to dislike drunks, who can be abusive and in a filthy physical condition. They wheeled him into a curtained-off room. When he started to come around, after vomiting and after being hooked up to an I.V. unit that fed fluids into his dehydrated system, he felt like he'd been run over by a train. His hands were trembling badly, he wasn't sure where he was, he had no memory of the evening, and perhaps most frightening of all, he thought he saw small animals in the room with him. "I thought I was going crazy." He was relieved when the same doctor who had seen him a month previously entered the room. In answer to Henry's questions, he told him that he had a condition known as D.T.s (delirium tremens), which accounted for his tremors and hallucinations. They were a clear sign that his alcohol abuse had begun to affect his brain. His liver function tests also showed serious deterioration. "He told me that if I wanted to die, I was doing a pretty good job of it."

After treatment with tranquilizers, vitamins, and fluids, Henry's head cleared, but he felt miserable and overwhelmed with fear. He also felt isolated. No one knew he was in the hospital, and he doubted that anyone cared that he was. In the hours that followed, Henry began to confront himself by looking in that mythical mirror we all look into during the critical period of a crisis. He stared at a man whose personal myths had been built on someone else's dreams. He had given up a teaching job he had loved to fulfill his mother's message ("Make money") and his father's message ("Write a book"). The advertising career had supplied the money, but not the satisfaction he had found in teaching. As for the book, he finally questioned whether he could write it at all. Because his identity had been so firmly linked with becoming a novelist, these thoughts left him feeling rootless and hollow. Alone, he confronted his worst fear: that he was a drunk and a loser.

New Beginnings

After two days of treatment and looking every one of his forty-five years and then some, Henry was released from the hospital with a list of phone numbers for alcohol treatment programs and Alcoholics Anonymous. He took the train home and went for a walk in the woods. In contrast to what he had been feeling in the hospital, he was now starting to feel a kind of release. Facing up to his deficiencies as a writer and the roles his parents played in shaping his dreams was, in effect, freeing him from living a lie. On his solitary hike, he acknowledged that his life had ground to a halt: he was an alcoholic, in poor health, alone, jobless, and facing drunk-driving charges. Yet he began to believe that he could turn his life around, that he didn't have to repeat the alcoholic histories of his father and grandfather. The data suggests that alcoholism has some hereditary characteristics, but this is by no means the whole story. In Henry's case, being raised in a family where alcohol was a dominant influence was a clear factor in determining his behavior.

As he began to let the novel go and accepted the fact that he had a drinking problem, "I felt like this enormous burden had been taken from me." Giving up his dreams of becoming a novelist was, in many ways, the easier of Henry's two problems to address. In the next few days, he questioned whether it was the right decision and always arrived at the same conclusion: being a novelist no longer "felt right." Drinking was another matter entirely. "I badly wanted a drink. If my license hadn't been suspended and the car totalled, I think I would have been out that door and at the pub in a matter of minutes." Fortunately, there wasn't any alcohol in the house. In the main, he had confined his drinking to bars, and what liquor there had been at home had been consumed before his accident. As the urge to drink became stronger with each passing hour, Henry accepted that it was not going to go away on its own. He needed help.

The phone numbers that the doctor had given him at the hospital were still in his overcoat pocket. He found the slip of paper and stared at the number for Alcoholics Anonymous for a long time before he went to the phone. Until now, Henry had never asked people for help with his personal problems. Ironically, alcohol had been his "helper" whenever he had needed to feel better. "I didn't want to phone AA, because I wasn't sure what I was going to find there. I knew the program had a religious facet to it, and except for a brief moment in the hospital when I had actually asked God for help — much to my amazement — I had never been religious." He hung up three times before he finally allowed the voice at the other end to make a connection with him.

Henry's first AA meeting was that evening in the basement of a local community center. The coordinator, who was a man his own age, picked him up from his home. Anticipating a room full of "down-and-outers," he was surprised to find a wide variety of people of all backgrounds and ages quietly chatting together before the meeting started. A former neighbor approached him and with a smile welcomed him to AA.

Many treatment programs and self-help groups follow the Alcoholics Anonymous model. AA is a worldwide, nonprofit organization that holds regular meetings. Its members use their first names only and follow a twelve-step program to recovery. The first step is "We admitted we were powerless over alcohol — that our lives had become unmanageable." The program concentrates on members helping other members abstain from alcohol for life. In addition to this strong sense of communality that AA encourages, there is also an intense spiritual aspect. The second and third steps are: "We came to believe that a power greater than ourselves could restore us to sanity," and "We made a decision to turn our will and our lives over to the care of God as we understood him."

At Henry's first meeting, members talked openly about their pasts and where they were on the road to recovery. Their stories were all variations on a theme: how alcohol had perpetuated false beliefs they had about themselves, how its disinhibiting effect had led them to irresponsible acts and the self-hatred that resulted from their terrible behavior, how it had brought them and the people they loved pain and despair. "I could identify with much of what they were saying. I still had a few problems with the religious aspect of it, but, all in all, that first meeting was a wonderful experience." When it was over, Henry met his sponsor or partner, an accountant named Tony. If Henry felt like a drink or just needed to talk, he was to call Tony.

In the weeks that followed, Henry phoned Tony often. He also attended three or four AA meetings a week. The meetings soon became an indispensable part of his life. He left them filled with resolve and feeling good about himself. This "first blush" of excitement is not unusual in the first weeks of membership in any intense ideological group system. Members, who are initially heavily involved in the process, often see the group as the answer to all their problems. This fervency usually modifies over time as a more realistic perspective takes hold.

After a few months of being a "true believer," and concentrating on little else, some disturbing facts of life began to intrude on Henry's initial euphoria. He was rapidly running out of money; his severance pay had been spent on mortgage payments, child support, lawyer's fees for his court case, and living expenses. When he wasn't at AA meetings, he was bored and lonely. The community work that he was required to do as a requirement of his parole had not begun yet, and he hesitated to phone old friends. One afternoon, the phone rang. Expecting a sales pitch or a wrong number, Henry was pleasantly surprised to hear

Meg's voice instead. She asked if she could come to visit. "After the way I had treated her over the years, I was touched when she told me she had kept in touch with my mother and knew about my going to AA. I was surprised that she still cared."

That evening Henry discussed his feelings with his wife for the first time in their marriage. He apologized for the past and realized, without saying anything to her, that he wanted her to be a part of his future. Meg admitted that she had missed him terribly. When she was leaving, they held each other tightly and agreed to meet again the following night. The next evening it was Meg's turn to share her feelings. She had been questioning why she had been so passive during their marriage, why she hadn't demanded that he stop drinking, and why she had blamed herself for it. Her questions were typical of a co-dependent, a person who through many years of tolerance of an addicted person's destructive behavior enters into a kind of subtle encouragement of the problem. In the process, their own lives are nearly destroyed because their entire identity becomes directed in the service of maintaining the family's equilibrium. The addiction goes on and on relentlessly, and the co-dependent becomes an accessory to the fact. There is an offshoot of Alcoholics Anonymous called Al-Anon, which is a program for people who have a relative or friend who is an alcoholic. Henry gave her a number to call and Meg began attending meetings. (There is also another branch of AA called Al-Teen for adolescent children of alcoholics, who often endure severe emotional pain and sadness.)

Both Henry and Meg were now involved in a healing process. As both became stronger within themselves over the following months, they became closer. It was clear to both of them, though unspoken as yet, that they were building a foundation for the type of marriage they had never had, one built on mutual respect, trust, and love.

Henry began looking for a job teaching again. His community service work had involved tutoring mature students, and it had reawakened his interest in teaching. The writing was not totally abandoned. As part of his recovery, he began keeping a journal. Journal writing is a wonderful way to express your feelings, frustrations, and hopes. The simple act of writing down what one is experiencing inside is a cleansing and rewarding activity. The journal itself becomes a cherished record of one's progress. "Ironically, some of my best writing is in that book, because I'm finally in touch with myself and those around me."

Five Years Later

I was introduced to Henry by a mutual friend six years after he had stopped drinking. He and Meg are now living together. Meg had moved back into their home about a year after they had resumed their relationship. This time their lives away from work are spent in pursuing common pastimes rather than solely individual ones. They attend plays and concerts together, and Henry is teaching Meg how to play tennis.

Henry is now the chairman of the Media Arts Department in a community college, where he can combine his advertising and administrative skills with his love of teaching. He is seeing his twenty-year-old daughter on a fairly regular basis and has resumed friendships that were lost during his drinking days. Alcoholics Anonymous is still an important part of his week. The spiritual dimension of the meetings, which once made him uncomfortable, has now been incorporated into his own life. "Looking back at the beginning of my journal, I can barely recognize the person I was then. I'll admit there are days when I could still use a drink. That's something I'll always have to struggle with, but when I think of the alternatives, it's well worth it."

Part Three

The Late Life Quest

T ypically, we tend to think of people reaching the third stage of life at age sixty-five, but again this is a rather meaningless cutoff. A person's psychological age can't be determined strictly by chronological age. One seventy-five-year-old I know refused a friend's invitation to go on a bus tour because she likes her independence and refuses to be shepherded around with "a bunch of old people." Her friend, on the other hand, likes the camaraderie and convenience of this way of travel and thinks the other woman should realize she's not getting any younger and "act her age."

Both of these women have accepted the common fallacy that all people in this age group are alike. The first woman is proud of the fact that she is "young-thinking" and dreads being associated with a group of "old fogies" even more than she dislikes the mode of transportation. She immediately assumes that no one in the group will have anything in common with her. The second woman knows this to be untrue, but leaves no room for her friend's preference for independent sightseeing. She believes her friend is unwise to travel alone "at her age."

The problem with looking at someone solely on the basis of chronological age is that we build in expectations and demands that may be inappropriate for a large number of people. We end up ignoring the fact that in the senior years, there are probably more discrepancies between people than in any other age group simply because of this population's widely different life experiences. A number of myths arise out of the "all older people are alike" fallacy. These include "all elderly people are miserable," "all people over the age of sixty-five want to retire," "seniors don't have sexual relationships," and "all older people lose their ability to reason." The first three obviously don't apply to every senior, and as for the fourth, the majority of people over the age of eighty can reason just as well as younger people; they just don't do it as quickly.

The problem with such myths is that some of us when we reach this stage of life begin to believe them ourselves. As in adolescence and midlife, the later years involve a number of tasks. Accepting invalid myths about ourselves, such as "I'm useless because I'm old," can be self-perpetuating and can interfere with the successful completion of these tasks of later life. For those who haven't yet built strong emotional foundations, the combination of myths about aging, personal myths held over a lifetime, and the often difficult tasks of this stage can be devastating. For example, if a person has always defined himself as an independent person, it is difficult to accept help from others when ill health strikes. Learning to be dependent on others for the first time since childhood is a task that men, in particular, can find challenging. The flip side is maintaining one's autonomy, which can also be challenging in the face of well-meaning but sometimes misinformed relatives — "But Aunt Bea, you know you shouldn't be living alone at eighty."

Another task of this age group is learning to live with the past. To the eternal questions "Who am I?" and "Where am I going?" is added the question "Where have I been?" We look back over our lives and, if we are to find inner peace, must come to terms with our losses and unachieved dreams as well as take pleasure in our successes. To reach this stage in life still burdened with a loss that occurred many years before robs us of peace of mind and limits our options in later life. I'm not talking about missing someone who has died or left. What I'm referring to is living in the past rather than the present, as in "If only my husband or wife were alive, I could do such-and-such," or "No matter how much I want to, I can never forgive my brother for that terrible argument we had."

Tied in with learning to live with past losses is adapting to present losses. This includes the loss of family and friends through illness, divorce, or death, as well as the loss of our own health. Each can precipitate a crisis. Death and illness, although obviously distressing, are at least expected at this stage in life. Divorce, on the other hand, can seem to come out of the blue and may deal a destructive blow to the self-esteem and sense of belonging of the spouse who is left behind. In both cases, older people mourn the loss of their life partners and, more often than not, they mourn being left alone.

Another loss in this age group is the loss of our careers. Adjusting to retirement can also have a negative impact on our self-esteem and sense of belonging, especially if the first is based on achieving certain goals at work and the second is based on friendships that don't extend outside the work-place. This is particularly true of sixty-five-year-old men who have not planned for their retirement and is increasingly true of women. Women, however, seem more adept at forming new relationships and retaining old ones than men and seem to be less rigidly defined by their previous roles. A man's sense of himself can often be rooted in the power and productivity he derives from his work. Take these away and he can feel without purpose and power.

The way we handle each of these tasks and the crises that may accompany them depends on a number of factors. How well we take care of our bodies is one. Those who safeguard their physical health as much as possible by eating properly, exercising, and having regular medical checkups tend to be better prepared to cope with the problems of later life. How well we maintain our emotional health by cultivating friendships and family ties, believing in something that gives meaning to our days, and getting involved in life outside the four walls of our living rooms is equally important. Unfortunately, not having enough money to live comfortably can negatively affect both of these factors. It is a sad comment on our society that many single elderly people, especially women, live below the poverty line, with the result that their mental and physical well-being is placed at risk.

When faced with crisis, some of us in this age group use destructive escape routes that have worked for us in the past to dull our emotional pain. Because overwork or promiscuity may no longer be possible as ways to avoid facing our problems, many elderly people turn to drugs. Alcohol is abused in this age group as it is in others, and prescription drugs, such as tranquilizers, or over-the-counter medication, such as painkillers, often take the place of street drugs.

When these escape attempts fail, as they inevitably do, a rising number of older people, particularly in the over-eighty group, are committing suicide. Although it may be less in comparison to the other age groups, the fact that it is increasing is cause for concern. Too many older people today feel they are superfluous members of society. The pressure on them not to become a burden to friends or relatives can be overwhelming and turning their lives around at this stage in life may seem like an impossible task.

Happily, it isn't. With the help of others, by finding that hidden core of confidence or courage within them, and by letting go of negative emotions, people of any age can overcome crisis and go on to lead enriched lives. In the later years, moving away from the success myths of middle age and the negative myths of old age toward caring for oneself and other people and toward an exploration of one's spirituality is an important part of this learning and healing process. There are a number of community and social programs set up to assist us along the way, from meal delivery and visiting homemakers' programs to community medical services to social activities such as square dances and bicycle tours. Your local family services agency is a good place to begin investigating these resources.

Before I introduce you to Carol and Jack in the next two chapters, I'd like to tell you about two couples I know. I recently attended the funeral of a friend's father. He had died of a degenerative spinal condition, which had left him partially disabled and in pain for the past ten years of his life. His wife had died two years previously of a nervous disorder, which had eventually paralyzed her. Throughout their years of failing health, this courageous couple had comforted each other with the wit and good humor that had marked their lives. As long as they were able, they continued the activities that had given them enjoyment — dining out, entertaining friends, attending church functions, and fund-raising. When they were no longer able to function on their own, they reached out for help. Not surprisingly, the many friends they had assisted in the past rallied round, enabling them to stay in the home they loved.

My friend stood up at the funeral and, on behalf of his father, thanked the many friends and family members who had assisted his parents over the years. Then he said, "I suspect that most of us feel we should be thanking him rather than the other way around. This is a service of thanksgiving. I want to thank my father for giving me the gift of his faith in life and God; for his understanding and willingness to listen; for always knowing the right thing to say at the right time; for his love that never wavered; and for his wonderful sense of humor, especially that twinkle in his eye just before a droll remark." What better legacy could this man have left his son?

After the funeral, I found myself thinking about another older couple I know. They have been blessed with relatively good health, yet each little pain is grumbled about. They are comfortably well off, but begrudge each dime spent on anything other than the necessities of life. They have each other, but their lack of respect and caring for the other is sad to see. In short, they are miserable people made more miserable by the fact that their negative attitude toward life and aging keeps family and friends away. I'm sure they would think Manya Joyce, the American woman who went parachuting for the first time in 1991 to celebrate her eighty-sixth birthday and to raise money for the Senior Olympics, was crazy or a foolish old lady or both. Their own bitterness blinds them to the joy that other people their age find in life and that could be theirs if they only reached out to find it.

At this stage of life, we have a choice. We can give up and wait for death, or we can continue on our quest, still open to the possibilities and learning experiences that surround us. I do not wish to pretend for a moment that aging is "easy," or that there are not inevitable experiences of deterioration and loss, both minor and major. But the response of many elderly people within their limitations varies tremendously. I have been truly inspired by older people who, in spite of severe physical and emotional setbacks, have continued to live life fully. To the extent that we can still function, aging is what we make of it. Not all of the obstacles it may bring need stop us from growing; many can be turned toward further growth or regeneration.

9. The Shock of Divorce

WITH HER ERECT BEARING, IMPECCABLE DRESS, and manners of a bygone era, Carol Lewis would have been described as a "real lady" by my mother. At sixty, after thirty-seven years of marriage, she was looking forward to her husband Ed's retirement. Throughout her life she had felt that everything she did was for other people — her parents, her husband, her children, her friends. Now pressures on her to perform and Ed to produce would diminish. Although they were an unlikely couple, with little in common, she hoped that retired life would improve their relationship.

They had met in her hometown, where Carol's father was a wealthy businessman. Her mother was one of those quiet women who fuss over their domineering husbands. Like most of the women of her generation, she raised her daughter to be a helpmate for a future husband. More emphasis was placed on pouring tea properly than schoolwork; nevertheless, Carol did well in school. She was particularly talented in art and after graduation attended an art college for a year and a half. It was while she was in college that her father introduced her to Ed.

Ed came from a working-class background. Street smart and determined to improve his lot in life, he had worked his way through university and had found a good job in the financial sector after graduation. He had met with Carol's father to discuss some financing for a joint project. The older man had been impressed by his young visitor's intelligence and ambition and had invited him home for dinner. At nineteen, Carol was bright, pretty, quiet, and somewhat insecure. At twenty-three, Ed was good-looking, aggressive, and self-assured. They seemed, in her parents' eyes at least, to be a good match and were thrown together at every opportunity — family get-togethers, formal parties, picnics by the pool. "Dad had a way of looking at him and then whispering to me, 'That boy's going to make some lucky girl a great husband some day.' Wink. Wink."

Carol wasn't so sure. On the one hand, she admitted to herself that Ed was attractive and was obviously going to be a success. Although her own family had not lost all of its money during the Depression, other families she knew had, and the comfort of a secure future with Ed was a strong point in his favor. On the other hand, she didn't love him and knew that her ideas about art and literature would always be only politely acknowledged by a man whose interests lay elsewhere. When she confided her worries to her father, he laughed at her concerns, telling her that romantic love was "for the movies, not real life." In the end, she did what her father wanted her to do. When Ed asked her to marry him, she said yes.

Right from the beginning of their marriage, they lived quite separate lives. Carol found Ed dull and unimaginative. Although she admitted that he was "a good provider," as her father would say, his business accomplishments bored her and he had no other interests. Throughout their marriage, he was away on business for long periods of time. She became accustomed to, and even enjoyed, his long absences. When he was home, she complained that "even when he was there, he wasn't." While Carol planned hospital benefits in one corner of their large Victorian house or fussed over the extensive gardens on the property, Ed worked in his study on the third floor.

Predictably, their sexual relationship was unsatisfactory for both of them. After the couple's two sons, Allan and Michael, were born, they seldom made love. Carol knew that Ed considered her sexually unresponsive and for many years had accepted this as fact. A passionate affair in the fifteenth year of their marriage changed her thoughts about her sexual self. She had met André, a French arts professor on sabbatical, at a party. A friendship formed and common interests quickly turned to love. Carol remembers this period as one of the happiest of her life. "I was deeply in love. Life was exciting and full, but I never thought about leaving Ed. You just didn't do that back then. Besides, I knew André would be going back to his own family at the end of the two years."

After nearly four decades of marriage, Carol didn't expect to find happiness in retirement, but she did look forward to the rewards that she felt were her due — travel with Ed, a more relaxed life style, new friendships. They had recently sold their house and moved into a beautiful three-bedroom condominium in another city. Ed had transferred the head office of his company and wanted to oversee the transition before his retirement. Carol hadn't objected. "I felt ready for a change. I didn't question his decision to move because essentially it was a business decision and I didn't have anything to do with his business." After the move, the squabbles that had marked her relationship with Ed seemed to diminish. They went out occasionally. There was no pressure to make love, particularly now that they had separate bedrooms. They had their health, and for their age, both were strikingly attractive. Their sons were both married and had good jobs. Life, if not full, was pleasant and predictable.

Heading for a Fall

Carol had always been pragmatic and philosophical. She accepted her role in life as Mrs. Edward Lewis. She had been groomed for the part and she felt she played it well. Although her marriage gave her little satisfaction, she never seriously thought about abandoning it. Her reasons were the same ones that many people give for staying in a bad relationship. At first, it was "for the children" and "because her parents, friends, and society as a whole frowned upon divorce." Later in life, as several of the couples she and Ed knew divorced, it was "for security" and "because divorce hadn't seemed to solve all of her friends' problems." Sadly, her complete acceptance of her role of wife and mother had meant that she had buried her own abilities and needs over the years and, in the process, had perpetuated a personal myth about herself.

The term "hot-house flower" is almost an anachronism today, but in Carol's youth it was in common usage. Carol saw herself as this type of woman — a sensitive, beautiful "girl" in need of protection and assistance. Throughout her childhood, her father had given her the message that women didn't count, that their needs and talents were secondary to those of men. Ed helped perpetuate this myth of the weak, helpless woman by taking care of all the household finances and providing her with nannies, housecleaning staff, and other workers to ensure a life of ease. Although she knew early in their marriage that Ed "wasn't my cup of tea," Carol, with no marketable skills, always felt ill equipped to handle life on her own. Like many women of her generation, she believed she needed a man to take care of her.

As they settled into their new home, Carol began to make plans for the future. She missed her friends, but couldn't honestly say that she missed the volunteer work she had done for years. There was a certain sameness to her old life, a going-through-the-motions quality, that she now had the opportunity to change. How much of a change there would be became apparent one month short of her sixty-first birthday. Ed arrived home one night after a week away on business and announced that he had fallen in love and was leaving Carol. "Thirty-seven years of marriage didn't seem to count for anything. It was totally unbelievable to me."

As Ed packed his suitcases in the bedroom, Carol alternated between feeling shattered, furious, and panic-stricken. It had never occurred to her that Ed would break their marital vows, which in her mind amounted to a contract in which he promised to take care of her and she in return promised to be his dutiful wife. The fact that their marriage had been devoid of any romance or spirit was seen by Carol as the rule rather than the exception in the marriages she knew. She thought he had felt the same. In an attempt to understand, she accused him of running off with someone younger and prettier, but was surprised to learn that his new-found love was actually older than Carol and from the same social circle. In some ways, this added to her sense of betrayal. In her "golden years," someone else would be enjoying the peace, status, and stability that were rightfully hers.

Hitting Rock Bottom

After Ed walked out the door with muttered reassurances that she'd "be fine," Carol collapsed on the sofa and, after hours of crying, fell asleep. She woke up in the middle of the night with a headache and that strange sense that she had had a bad dream, only to remember that it wasn't a dream. In the hours until daybreak, she tried to think rationally about what to do, but couldn't get past her fear and anger. "I was unraveling at the seams. I truly believed that my life had ended." As the days went by, Carol at first refused to accept that the separation had occurred. "I tried to convince myself that it was temporary. He would be back. I didn't even know how to write a cheque. I simply couldn't imagine living on my own. It was just too terrifying to contemplate."

We all can cope better with life's problems if they consist of something we can fight for, or protect, or run from. In Carol's case, she was thrust into a world of ambiguity where nothing was safe, controllable, or predictable any longer. Her emotional foundations had been pulled out from under her in one short evening and didn't serve her well in the weeks that followed. An already low self-esteem plunged lower. Her sense of belonging was intricately tied to her role of wife, which had been taken from her, and she didn't have a spiritual base to fall back on in times of need. For many women in Carol's situation, there is an overwhelming sense that they have wasted their lives caring for their husbands. Usually, they have already had difficulty adjusting to their children leaving home. When their husbands do the same, they experience a devastating sense of betrayal and loss of identity.

"For days I felt like he had kicked me in the stomach. I could physically feel it." I have heard this metaphor on many occasions. People who are devastated by unexpected news actually "feel" a spot in the center of their upper abdomens where the pain localizes itself. Psychologically stressful events can affect our physical well-being in a variety of ways. We can experience headaches, backaches, nausea, and a number of other physical expressions of our inner pain.

When Carol began to accept that Ed was gone for good, her thoughts centered, not on killing herself, but killing Ed. "I did think once or twice about suicide and then I would think how convenient that would be for Ed, and I'd work myself into a rage." She felt that if he had left her when she was still beautiful and young, perhaps her life would have been different. Maybe she could have started over with someone new. Her anger toward her husband left her exhausted. She couldn't eat or sleep and spent her time wandering through the rooms of the lavish apartment, which she now detested for the lost life it represented. Knowing that she wasn't capable of killing herself or her husband, she felt powerless. There didn't seem to be any way to escape or any way to strike out at the man who she felt had ruined her life.

Actually, there was one way Carol hoped to hurt him and, in the process, relieve some of the stress she was under. Like many of us in crisis, she fell back on an old behavioral pattern. In the past, when something had upset her, she had gone shopping. This time, she drove to the most expensive shopping area in the city and went on a buying spree with Ed's credit cards. "I'll get him in his bank book," she thought. It was a futile attempt. She didn't feel any better by the time she got home, and her guilt-ridden spouse didn't say a word about it when he received the bills a month later.

Although Carol knew she needed help, she didn't know where to turn. The day after Ed left, she had phoned Allan and Michael. They hadn't seemed surprised by her news,

and she suspected Ed had already discussed his plans with
them. They offered her their support, but because they
lived miles away, there was little of a practical nature that
they could do. "I knew they were sincere, but I couldn't help
but wonder what their father had said to them. Boys are
always closer to their dads. I hung up the phone feeling like
an outsider in my own family." She was embarrassed to
phone her out-of-town friends, for the sad reason that telling
them her husband had left her was an admission of failure.
She couldn't bear to think of the gossipy dissections of her
marriage that would follow her calls. Her pride wouldn't
allow her to pick up the phone.

Alone in her apartment, Carol began drinking heavily.
Her single evening cocktail became three and then four
cocktails. She got up later and later each day and sometimes
didn't bother to change out of her nightgown. The days
began to run into each other, each one the same as the last,
filled with self-hate and hatred toward Ed.

Three months after the separation, she was walking
down the hall of the apartment on her way to the parking
garage and met Mindy, a neighbor on the same floor. Mindy,
a well-to-do woman who had never married, was little more
than an acquaintance, so Carol was surprised when she
stopped her in the hall and asked her to go with her to high
holiday services. Although Carol and Ed had both been
raised in nominally Jewish homes, their families had never
celebrated Jewish holidays. As a child, she remembered
being invited once with her family to a passover seder,
which she found boring. After their children were born, the
Lewises occasionally went to temple on the high holidays,
but this was purely for show, as upstanding members of the
community. If anything, her recent experiences had re-
affirmed her conviction that a caring God didn't exist, and
her initial reaction to Mindy's invitation was to turn her

down. Her friendly neighbor, however, was insistent, and Carol didn't have the energy to argue with her. "I also knew I had to get out, even if it was with someone I barely knew or even wanted to know."

The services were held in a Unitarian Church, which was rented by a small group of people who formed a temporary congregation each year during the high holidays. As the service began, Carol found herself moved by it in a way she had never experienced before. Even the rabbi's sermon seemed to speak to her directly. Rabbi Mandelcorn was a frail man of seventy whose hands trembled, but he spoke on helping yourself and others with an impassioned and forceful voice. Although Carol knew he was retired and only held these services once a year, she introduced herself after the service and asked if he would meet with her. I suspect that he agreed to see her because, from the little she told him that day, he could see the troubled soul under the poised exterior.

Two days later, over a cup of coffee in a local restaurant, Rabbi Mandelcorn listened as Carol described her past life and the miserable existence she now led. He showed considerable interest but little sympathy. "He told me that here I was with so much to offer the world and all I could do was moan and groan about the wrong turn my life had taken. I think at that point I needed someone to say 'Get on with your life,' and that's exactly what he did." Carol found herself admitting that, yes, she had been totally wrapped up in her own problems. Not missing a beat, the rabbi invited her to participate in a monthly Bible study class. Carol laughed. "I wasn't ready for that yet, but I thanked him for listening and for giving me some much-needed advice."

A sensitive spiritual adviser or counselor is often crucial in "reprogramming" our lives. At times he or she not only serves as a spiritual guide, but may also be capable of giving psychotherapeutic support. The two approaches do not preclude each other; in fact, they are often intertwined. A strong belief system may figure in the regeneration equation, and a spiritual approach can be vital in encouraging this.

Losses must be grieved, and this is what Carol had been doing for the past few months. Her feelings of denial, anger, sadness, and fear are common feelings for those who have lost a mate. In her case, these feelings were compounded by her perception of herself as someone who was unable to face life on her own. In the critical period we all reach in times of crisis, Carol's moment of truth came after her meeting with Rabbi Mandelcorn. She began to look at herself and her marriage with a kind of clarity that had eluded her all her life.

Without forgiveness, it is difficult for any of us to move forward. Forgiving others, forgiving God, but most of all forgiving ourselves, is a necessary part of the healing process. Although Carol was still angry at Ed, when she looked objectively at their marriage, she could see that she was as much to blame for its ending as Ed was. She hadn't loved him. Their marriage had been a sham. As for herself, she had been too involved in playing roles to reach inward to find herself and outward to find other people. It was time she did both.

New Beginnings

For some of the women in the Lewises' social milieu, volunteering one's time to various charitable causes was done out of a sense of social correctness rather than any overriding sense of helping the less fortunate. In the past, Carol had fallen into this category. Now she decided she would phone the city's volunteer bureau or the Jewish Family Services to genuinely offer her services to those who had much less in the way of money, support, or health. She also had another look at a brochure of extension courses at the local community college, which had been dropped into her mailbox a few days earlier. There was an interior decorating course that looked interesting.

Like many people, though, Carol found the transition period between thinking about changing her life and actually doing something about it difficult to bridge. Weeks passed before she found the courage to act. Her children were particularly encouraging about her going back to school, and she had been proud when she originally told them about her plans, but within a day or two she had been filled with self-doubt. The course entailed two two-hour evening courses a week from January to August. "I hadn't sat in a classroom for years. I had absolutely no faith at all in my own abilities. I worried about keeping up with the other students." Finally, on the last day of registration, she signed up for the course.

Her fears turned into panic when she walked into her first class. There was no one her own age or even approaching her age. The students were, for the most part, as young or younger than her own children. She was about to turn around and leave when the teacher, a dark-haired man in his mid-thirties, walked up to her and said, "You must be Mrs. Lewis. I'm Chris." Her birth date on the registration form had obviously alerted him that an older woman would be in his class. As he invited her to take a seat, Chris whispered, "Frankly I was expecting someone who looked a lot older. I must tell you I really admire you for going back to school at your age. You're one gutsy lady." Touched by his warm remarks, she took a seat in the center of the classroom.

The taste and style that was evident in Carol's own home served her well in her classes. She had a natural talent for putting together colors and materials in a striking way, and soon the other students were asking her opinion of their own work. She felt they and Chris genuinely liked and respected her and, occasionally, she went out for a drink after class with "her kids" as she called them. For those two evenings a week, she felt good about herself. The rest of the week was still a problem.

Between classes, Carol slipped back into self-doubt and self-recrimination. She punished herself for not pursuing her own interests earlier in her life. And she blamed herself, on the one hand, for not working on her marriage, and on the other hand, for not leaving Ed many years before. This belief in her own inadequacy prevented her from doing any volunteer work. It also brought a sense of futility. "Even if I did finish the course, I didn't think anyone would hire me at my age."

And she was lonely. Like many women her age, Carol had never lived alone. It's true that she had lived on her own while Ed was away on business, but she had always known that she was part of a couple. There was an alternative to being alone, perhaps not a very satisfactory one, but an alternative just the same. She had felt like a social pariah since the separation. This is not an unusual feeling for recently separated men and women. Friends often don't know what to do or whom to side with or what to say. In confusion, many simply withdraw from both former spouses at the very time when their needs are greatest. A few of Carol's friends from her former hometown had phoned or written after hearing the news of the separation via the grapevine. They had expressed their dismay and support but hadn't extended any firm invitations to visit. "Talking on the phone has never been my strong point, particularly when the topic is such a personal one. I didn't feel comfortable phoning them back. They had their own lives and I didn't fit in any more."

It was Chris who picked up on her sense of isolation and became a friend. They occasionally had coffee together on their own after class and once in a while he would drop over to Carol's apartment to visit if he had a client in the neighborhood. "I was surprised when he told me he was a homosexual. I'd never met one before, and I found it amusing that my first friend in the city would be someone whom I wouldn't have had anything to do with in my old life." It was Chris who suggested that she look into a singles club run by the Y. His Aunt Mary, who was slightly older than Carol, was a regular participant and loved going. A few short weeks ago, Carol would have found such an idea distasteful, but, as she told Chris, "beggars can't be choosers." In the past, she would also have worried about the difference in social class between some of the other members and herself. Beginning a new life, however, has a way of changing old prejudices and opening our eyes to new possibilities. Carol decided to give the club a try.

Carol went to two get-togethers with Mary, a warm, talkative, fun-loving sort of woman. Unfortunately, she found them painfully awkward. None of the men who approached her to chat or dance interested her in the least. She classified all of them as "losers," which was a throwback to her old snobbish self. Although she was able to override her initial reactions to the club in order to attend, once there and thrust into a threatening situation, the negative thoughts of a lifetime took over. This isn't uncommon. The more insecure we are ourselves in a situation, the more we see the blemishes and deficiencies of others. Unlike Mary, who seemed to be having a good time, the quiet and demure Carol found the whole affair demeaning. The second time she went, she lasted one hour before taking a cab home early.

Mary was the one bright spot in this upsetting experience. Her bubbly personality seemed to complement Carol's, and they became good friends. They shared a number of interests as well as a self-deprecating wit. One evening they were watching a sitcom on television. The plot revolved around a therapy group for people who were newly single, and Carol asked Mary if she knew of a similar group in their city. "Mary didn't know of one, and wasn't interested herself — she'd been on her own for years — but it looked like the kind of group I would feel comfortable in. I didn't need to dance. I needed to talk!"

Finding the group was another story. She spent hours on the phone calling one social agency and religious group after the other, until finally she learned of a group which met weekly in a church basement. In spite of its venue, it was a secular group organized by the Family Service Agency, an international social agency that counsels families in trouble. Even before she went to her first meeting, Carol was proud of herself for having the perseverance to keep looking and for resolving the problem on her own.

At her first meeting, she was relieved to see that most of the people there were around her own age. She found that she felt more comfortable talking in this group than in her class or at the singles club, and although the discussions held at the meetings were an important part of the group's agenda, Carol was pleased to discover that the group also planned to hold social outings throughout the year.

By reaching out to others, coming to grips with her lifelong denial of her self-worth, and finding pursuits that would help define her own goals and needs in life, Carol was able to overcome her despair and despondency. She eventually noticed that she was no longer as lonely as she had been. "Life was good. Ironically, I realized I'd never been as lonely as when I had been married."

Five Years Later

Carol now lives in a more modest one-bedroom apartment in the same city. At age sixty-seven, she looks and feels wonderful, and even expresses gratitude to Ed for "saving her life." She works part-time for an interior decorator and part-time for an umbrella organization of social services, where she was instrumental in setting up a multilingual information and access service for senior citizens. Her circle of friends has widened, and although she has no one man in her life, she is frequently invited out for dinner or a show. Lately she has become more interested in spiritual issues and her own Jewish heritage, and these have added a comforting "new dimension" to her life. Most importantly, Carol feels optimistic about her future. She will do fine no matter what life brings.

10. The Myth of the Self-Sufficient Man

STANDING BEHIND THE COUNTER OF HIS SMALL hardware store for the last time, Jack Kalescha suddenly felt incredibly tired. The past few years had been tough going. Most of the former customers of his grandfather's old store had drifted away to the big chains with their larger and cheaper stocks. When they did come in, it was for odd parts that they hoped to find among the assorted tools, plumbing goods, and gardening supplies piled to the ceiling of the little store. When he couldn't find a buyer for the business, he had finally had to admit that he couldn't make a go of it any longer on his own. Reluctantly, and with some embarrassment, he followed his accountant's advice and declared bankruptcy. On the store's final day, this heavy-set, shortish man with the wiry white hair reflected that what he had liked best about his working life as a hardware retailer was the wonderful smell of all those myriad bits and pieces. He recalls thinking that this was a peculiar thing to anticipate missing. Jack knew carpentry and tools inside out and for years had taught his customers all about fixing and renovations. He would miss that role as teacher, too.

Looking back after he retired, Jack felt he had led a full life. Although he'd been forced to quit high school to help support his family, he'd accepted this because all his friends had had a similar share of hardships in those days. He was a well-read, self-taught man in many areas despite his lack of formal schooling. His marriage to Sara had lasted forty-eight years. His two children were now married themselves and living in other cities. They were "good kids," although now that he was no longer working, he felt a tinge of resentment and sometimes abandonment. "They don't have much time for us. They're too busy moving jobs, moving houses, always on the move. I stayed in one town all my life, but not them."

Over the years, Jack had weathered a number of crises, just as most people experience and endure in the course of a lifetime. Forty years ago, his second-born had died of crib death. Thirty years ago, he had had a brief affair. Sara had forgiven him, and their love had grown stronger after the pain of his betrayal had healed. His brother's premature death of a heart attack and his sister's battle with multiple sclerosis had also taken their toll. But of all the hardships Jack had had to endure, the one that seemed to bother him the most was his failure, through no fault of his own, to serve his country in war. He was too young for the First World War, and too old for the Second. This didn't stop him from pretending he had been in the military. As an outspoken and patriotic citizen, he felt that people would condemn him if they knew he hadn't seen action in any battle.

Throughout his life, when faced with adversity, Jack had prided himself on being a "rock" — strong, resourceful, and resilient. He let everyone know that he had never had to ask for help and "never had any use for people who accepted handouts and who weren't prepared to work for what they got." At sixty-seven, he was in relatively good health, owned his own home, had some savings in the bank, and with his social security pension, he and Sara would "make do." (Although even social security made him feel queasy because of its welfare connotations.)

For the next three years, Jack puttered around the house and did a few odd jobs for neighbors. All the renovations that he had done on his home over the years had stood the test of time. "Besides," he said, "why do anything to change the place now, when it's just two old people living here?" Other than reading, he had never developed any interests outside the business, but when Sara suggested he join a seniors' club at the community center down the street, he scoffed at the idea. He wasn't about to join a "club for old fools."

Heading for a Fall

Jack's pride in his self-sufficiency was vital to him, perhaps more important than anything else. He certainly emphasized his gung-ho philosophy of self-reliance and independence in many of his conversations. At seventy, when his health began to fail, as it inevitably does as we age, he denied that anything could be wrong. Like many people who have had the good luck to be healthy most of their lives, he insisted he had never been sick a day in his life. But when his headaches, fatigue, and occasional chest pain got worse rather than better, he had to admit that it was time to see a doctor. Jack's condition was diagnosed as high blood pressure, and he was immediately put on medication to lower it and given a mild tranquilizer to reduce stress. In addition, because his blood cholesterol level was also elevated, he was placed on a diet and exercise regimen.

For a man who had made his own decisions all his life, being told what to eat and how to exercise and what pills to take was deeply distressing. Just the idea of taking pills was anathema to him. Believing they were a "crutch," Jack had rarely used even painkillers over the years. At first, he refused to tell Sara why he had been at the doctor's — "just a little checkup" — but when she found the pills and threatened to call his doctor, he relented. It was hard to admit to her that her tough guy husband was no longer quite as tough as he used to be.

Although his blood pressure dropped considerably and his cholesterol level came down over a period of a few months, Jack began to have increasing bouts of shortness of breath and a vague "heaviness" or pressure on his chest after any kind of exertion. He tried to deny these problems, too, until he could no longer tolerate them. This time his doctor diagnosed angina pectoris. He was sent to a cardiologist, who prescribed nitroglycerin pills and further restricted and modified his diet — fewer calories, no fats, no salt, little alcohol, no smoking. Jack was angry at his doctor, who seemed to be denying him all of life's little pleasures. He had loved a few drinks of bourbon in the evening followed by a big fat stogie. This was an evening ritual of long duration which was going to be hard to give up. For someone who was always in control of his life, he seemed to be giving up that control and power to others, and he was increasingly resentful of their interference — as he perceived it.

It isn't unusual for those of us who have taken pride in our independence to become depressed when lifetime activities are severely limited. For Jack, it was especially difficult. Increasing lethargy, sadness, and insomnia plagued Jack for months before he was referred to a psychiatrist by his doctor. This was too much. He swore Sara to secrecy before he went and felt miserable sitting in the waiting room. Just seeing a "shrink" seemed such an admission of failure and inadequacy. During the session, as his personality, retirement, bankruptcy, and relationship with his family were raised as possible causes of his poor state of mind, Jack became further upset. When the psychiatrist wanted to add an anti-depressant to his drug intake, he responded with frustration and anger, "Is this all you guys know how to do, push pills?" He walked angrily out of the office, throwing the prescription into a garbage can on his way to the car.

His refusal to take this new medication proved to be a good decision. When Jack told his cardiologist that his depression had begun shortly after he had begun taking one of his medications, the doctor remembered that one of its side effects was occasional depression. Soon after the offending medication was changed, Jack's mood did lift considerably, but he couldn't seem to get back to where he had been before. One reason for his continuing unhappiness was another side effect of his medication — impotence. Although Sara was loving and understanding as always, Jack felt terrible. He and Sara had enjoyed a wonderful sex life. Not being able to make love was further proof of his failure as a man.

As his health problems accelerated, Jack withdrew from everyone, including Sara. He felt ashamed of his own physical and emotional vulnerabilities. When his chest pains became more severe and more incapacitating, he was admitted to hospital to find out the reasons for his increasing discomfort. What the cardiologists found was that years of eating fatty foods, long hours of hard work, overweight, smoking, and little exercise had all contributed to diffuse arteriosclerosis. Many of his arteries were clogged with fatty plaque. Tests showed that he needed a triple coronary bypass, which would involve transferring three healthy arteries from his leg to his heart, and an aortic valve replacement, which would replace the damaged heart valve with a new one. Both procedures would be done during the same operation. Jack and Sara were told there was some risk involved and there were no guarantees that the operation would cure his symptoms. This upset both of them, but because Jack could no longer move without considerable pain, he decided to go for broke and have the operation.

The day before the operation, he ruefully asked his doctor, "Why is this all happening to me now?" The omniscient practitioner immediately replied, "We pay for our excesses eventually." This comment reflected not only the doctor's insensitivity and arrogance, but also North American society's preoccupation with healthy living as a moral mandate. Jack recalls that he wanted to throttle "the s.o.b." but at that point in his life, he didn't have the energy to squash an ant. His vaunted pride in his strength was past the point of jeopardy. He felt beaten and humiliated.

Hitting Rock Bottom

Some older people actually like being in hospital. If their problems are fairly minor, they enjoy the change in routine, the attention they receive, and the absence of immediate responsibilities. For Jack, though, being in hospital was agony. He felt like a child, or sometimes barely human, as his body was poked and prodded by strangers. The post-operative period was particularly rocky. He had a couple of paroxysms of high blood pressure and a "bleed" at the site of the surgery, which meant further operating and a return to the Intensive Care Unit.

After his discharge from hospital four weeks later, his health began to slowly improve, but by this time, Sara had developed complications from her long-standing mild diabetes. Her eyesight was failing, and while she never complained about anything, he knew how unhappy and worried she was. When Marty, his lifelong friend, died suddenly of a massive heart attack, Jack felt he was being given a message from God. "I never had much use for organized religion, so I thought it was kind of odd that I had begun either blaming God for my problems or asking him to stop sending them to me. I just wanted to yell, 'Please stop!' "

They didn't stop. Sara's and his own health and their medical bills dominated his thoughts. When he wasn't worrying about them, he berated himself about past disappointments — his lack of financial success, the humiliation he had felt when he had declared bankruptcy, how little time he had spent with his children. Even keeping some small bit of income from the income tax department didn't escape his scrutiny. On hearing the news that his newborn grandson had been born with a condition called hydrocephalus, a blockage in the fluid absorption system of the brain, and needed a surgically placed catheter implanted immediately, Jack had had it. All the reassurances in the world — his son had arranged for the neurosurgeon to speak to his father personally by phone — did nothing to comfort him. He felt himself sinking deeper into depression.

Jack's rigid "go it alone" mentality put him at a distinct disadvantage when faced with the losses that are a part of this stage of life. The confident exterior that had covered his inner feelings of failure was crumbling to such an extent that he could no longer bear to face the world outside his home. Now when he opened the medicine cabinet to take yet another one of his seventeen pills a day, he considered taking a handful of them and ending it all. "All I could see was more pain and more loss ahead."

As badly as he felt psychologically, Jack noticed that his physical health was actually better. He could certainly do more now without any accompanying chest pressure or pain. A few weeks ago he had felt paralyzed. Now, ironically, he felt he had the energy to kill himself. The final straw came when Sara was hospitalized one cold, rainy morning. She had a bad case of blocked veins in her legs due to her diabetes. As Jack looked at her in the hospital bed, he was struck by how fragile she looked and was overcome by a sense of helplessness. There seemed to be nothing he could do to stop this string of disasters. Suicide appeared to be the only way out. "I wasn't good for anything or anyone at that stage in the game."

When Jack left the hospital after sitting with Sara for a few hours, she was in a deep sedated sleep. He had walked to the hospital, which wasn't far from their home, but instead of returning immediately to the house, he continued to walk through the rain. He remembered that he used to walk as a teen-ager when he wanted to figure something out. This time he was tired of thinking and worrying; he just wanted to get away from what had become a miserable existence. He was about to pass the community center, but then, almost on a whim, decided to take a look inside. "At least I could sit down," he recalls thinking with resignation. I'm sure his decision to enter a building that he would have been embarrassed to visit a couple of months before was partly to verify his steadfast belief that the seniors' group was full of dependent old has-beens and partly because he felt so tired and terribly lonely, although he wouldn't have admitted the latter. On another level, he felt that a look at the center would reinforce his determination to end his life. He was convinced, he told me, that it would be so depressing, so devastatingly decrepit, that he'd be resolved in his decision to end his life.

The seniors' group was a revelation to Jack. He hadn't expected to find such a wide range of ages. There were men and women there who looked younger and certainly in better health than he was. "I thought everybody would be sitting around in chairs sipping tea, I guess." Instead, he watched as people sculpted, painted, and played cards and chess. Feeling like an intruder, he was about to leave when a familiar voice called out to him. He was somewhat dismayed to see that it was a neighbor who had bored him repeatedly in the past with his tales of woe. Today, though, Alex seemed in fine spirits as he showed Jack the sculpture he was working on. Although he was no great shakes as a sculptor, he seemed to be enjoying himself immensely.

As they talked, Jack found himself repaying the Alex of old in kind. He unloaded all his recent problems, expecting to find a sympathetic ear from a fellow sufferer. You can imagine how annoyed he was when Alex proved to be only mildly sympathetic. "He told me life had a way of throwing curve balls at our age. Said everybody in the room had similar stories. Everybody there had suffered from illness and tragedy. At the time, I didn't feel like I needed a lecture from Alex of all people." As he attempted to say good-bye to the friendly sculptor, Alex interrupted and suggested he come in the next day to see the group's social worker, Mrs. Morrow. "Apparently she had helped him out after his wife had died."

Jack trudged home, still peeved at Alex's unasked-for advice but not feeling nearly as strongly about killing himself as he had been earlier in the afternoon. That evening he went to visit Sara. She was pleased when he told her where he had been that afternoon and delighted when he said he would be going back the next day. He couldn't believe what he was saying.

New Beginnings

That evening, for the first time in his life, Jack admitted to himself that he needed some help. He made up his mind to go and see the social worker Alex had talked about the next day. Sleeping soundly for the first time in a long while, he awoke with a sense of purpose rather than dread. Instead of putting on the old clothes he had taken to wearing day in and day out despite Sara's protests, he chose a new shirt and pair of pants she had given him for Christmas, had a decent breakfast, and walked down to the community center.

Debbie Morrow was a pleasant-looking woman in her mid-forties. She welcomed Jack warmly and invited him into her office in one corner of the busy center, where she listened intently and sympathetically to the list of calamities that had befallen him. Mixed in were protestations that he was different from the other people "out there" because he had always stood on his own two feet. Although she didn't disagree with this last point, Debbie did say that it was sometimes helpful to spend time with other people who had gone through similar difficulties. She invited him to stay the morning, but emphasized that there was no pressure on him to become involved with the group if he didn't want to be. In a couple of days she would be back at the center and invited him to come in for another talk.

Jack felt liked and understood by this "wonderful woman," as he later described her to Sara. He walked out of her office feeling better than he had in months, and when he was asked if he would like to join a gin rummy game, he jumped at the invitation. The men he played with were all strangers, but before long, he was having a terrific time with them. Since his friend Marty had died, Jack had kept to himself, and he now realized how much he had missed the companionship of other men his age.

In the next few days, Jack was astounded by how much better he felt. His problems, of course, didn't disappear, but he was no longer going over every real or imagined mistake he had ever made during his lifetime. He stopped railing against God and decided that he had to stop attacking himself, too, and get on with the business of living. Part of this healing process was rejoining the world. He called his children to tell them he was "back" and contacted a few friends and relatives he had lost touch with after his retirement.

Jack's optimism was short-lived. The wife of one of the old friends he had chatted with on the phone called to tell him that his friend had had a stroke and was paralyzed on the right side of his body. Jack's mood plummeted yet again. He dragged himself over to the community center and angrily told the card group about his latest bad news. He was given a great deal of support, but although everyone liked Jack, the "unfairness" he talked about didn't register with most of them. After he finished his story, the conversation drifted to other subjects, and one man began to tell how he and his wife got themselves out of bed in the morning. They both had had heart attacks and tended to be "stiff as boards" when they woke up. To get around this problem, the husband would push his wife over to the edge of her side of the bed, she would struggle into a sitting position, get up, walk around the bed, grab his hands, and haul him up into a sitting position. There was much kibitzing about this push and haul wake-up procedure, and Jack momentarily forgot his own problems.

During the next few weeks, Jack spent a lot of time with Debbie Morrow. In his early seventies, he was beginning to deal, not only with his recent difficulties, but also with problems that had beset him for more than half a century. We all indulge in considerable "acting" in our lives, pretending that all is well. Jack's personal myth was that he was a failure, a fourth-generation American who was still working class. This invalid myth had plagued Jack's life.

The dedicated pursuit of success, power and prestige reached its zenith in the heyday of the eighties, but it has always been a hallmark of the New World's way of life. Ron Bersani was the personification of that singularly directed zeal, also in a misguided and destructive way. Both used the pursuit of that image of success to avoid any examination of their concerns about themselves.

In talking with Debbie and looking at himself honestly, Jack learned that he didn't have to be a major success in business to like himself or to be seen as a worthwhile human being. Shedding the great independent and patriotic facade that had covered his low self-esteem enabled him to feel better about himself than he had felt all his life. The pretense that we are stronger and more confident than we actually are is extraordinarily common. It feels good to finally open up and admit failures and vulnerabilities.

Even at this relatively late stage of life, Sara, his friends, and Debbie Morrow could see changes in Jack's personality. He was much more relaxed and much more accepting of himself and others. Through the crises he had endured, he had become a different and happier man. He had discovered that he didn't have to prove that he could do everything alone and that he could accept the idea that he needed and could rely on other people.

Five Years Later

The Kaleschas sold their family home and moved into a two-bedroom seniors' apartment more suited to their life style and age. There they have more security, neighbors their own age, and free transportation downtown and to the community center, and also nursing help is available. Now that he tries to be honest with himself, Jack feels more at peace than ever before, although the losses and infirmities continue. The most difficult one for Jack and Sara has been Sara's almost total blindness due to complications of her diabetes. She is quite mobile in the apartment, but Jack is now in charge of cooking and cleaning and, with his wife's help from the sidelines, has become an accomplished cook.

The seniors' group at the community center is still an important part of Jack's life. He teaches carpentry there now and has become involved in a senior mentors program at a local school. Each term he and a young student work on a woodworking project together. "We build some pretty fancy stuff," he smiles. Reaching out to others for help and helping others in return has given Jack an inner strength that is much more satisfying to him than his old self's superficial strength and independence.

Epilogue

THE PEOPLE IN THIS BOOK, MYSELF INCLUDED, would tell you they are thankful, not for the enormous pain caused by the crises they survived, but for the way they were forced to make profound changes in their lives. In a curious way, crisis can often reveal inner strengths and resources we never knew we possessed. What this enabled them to do was to take control and face their personal myths and accompanying problems. They now feel they are moving forward in healthy and constructive directions rather than being mired in one spot or running to nowhere on an endless treadmill. They feel, often for the first time in their lives, true to themselves, to others, and to a higher value system.

This doesn't mean their lives, or mine for that matter, are now perfect. After his mother died, Henry went to a bar for an evening of drinking. Anna's self-pity and anger returned when she found out that a man she was dating was already married. Jack faltered when another of his friends became ill. Indeed, all of them have had to deal with new obstacles in the years since the initial crisis. What has changed is their

reactions to these new problems. Although their first response may be rooted in old patterns, their second — the
one they have come to trust — is based on their growing
inner strength and self-knowledge. They know they can
now reach within for help, and that in times of need, it's
permissible, and indeed wise, to reach out to others for help,
too.

There are a few red flags to watch for on the road to
recovery. One is the feeling that we are beginning to play a
role again that not only doesn't belong to us any more, but
also is one we know to be destructive. In some ways it feels
familiar and comfortable, but when we stand back, we realize that it is demoralizing. When this happens, it's time to re-
evaluate ourselves and our goals. Within the limits of our
abilities or circumstances, are we really doing what we want
to be doing with our lives? Do we really respect ourselves for
the way we are acting at this time? If not, what changes can
be made to get us back on track? How do we get out of our
own shadows and enter our inner light?

Another warning sign is the familiar feeling that a new
problem is painfully unique to us and that no one else will
understand. We feel increasingly alienated and estranged
from others. In fact, it's impossible to reinvent the wheel
where life's difficulties are concerned. There is always
someone, somewhere, who has experienced this kind of pain
and, more importantly, who will understand and help. By the
same token, let us always remember to be sensitive to the
needs of others who call out to us for help during times of
crisis.

A third warning sign is the return of an old feeling of
emptiness and dread. Overcoming crisis is not a guarantee
of constant happiness. Life has a way of throwing us curves
from time to time, which make us feel anxious and fearful.
Having once been in the depths of despair, we experience an

immediate, intense response of "Uh-oh, here we go again!"
If you feel fulfilled — that is, if you are true to yourself and
have a sense of what that means, if you feel part of a
community of people you like or love, and if you have values
or beliefs that are important to you — you don't need to feel
happy every waking moment (it's impossible anyway, unless
you have a serious mood disorder!). But there are times
when our emotional foundations seem to crumble, and
futility and depression may steal back into our lives. At the
first signs of their return, we need to ask ourselves what we
can do to bolster our sense of self-esteem, belonging, and
believing. Have we complimented ourselves lately for a job
well done? Can we find ways to spend more time with our
friends or family? Are we being true to ourselves?

What can we do to get back in touch with our spiritual
selves? Our quest for inner peace evolves as we grow older
and the circumstances of our lives change. Those people
who come closest to being truly happy men and women are
those who are able to nurture and further build upon their
emotional foundations. Their sense of who they are becomes stronger, in that they can better withstand adversity,
and at the same time gentler, in the sense that their capacity
for forgiveness and acceptance of self and others has grown.
Masks and games of deception or manipulation are no
longer needed. In this inner place of refuge and love there is
a sense of authenticity, which brings meaning and purpose
to life.

What do I want to leave you with? The simple fact that we
are all in this together. That life is a struggle at times for all
of us. That there is a community of "humanitas," which
supports the rejuvenation of individual lives. Most importantly, I hope that you have been able to sense the extraordi-
nary resilience of ordinary human beings, like you and me.

The nine people in this book are not superhuman. Nor do they exhibit extreme pathological behavior. They are everyday individuals who have gone through a period of crisis that challenged the foundations of their lives; indeed, most of them considered suicide at some point. They are not victims of natural disasters or historical forces. Instead, they are the victims of their own fears, frailties, and self-fulfilling prophecies. They are, like many of us, people who developed destructive, invalid myths about themselves, myths that negatively programmed their attitudes to all activities in their lives. Eventually, the dissonance between the roles they were playing and their true selves drove them into a state of crisis.

It is at that point of no return that they discovered the existence of their dormant souls. After years of looking in that metaphoric mirror, seeing only cosmetic illusions, they were able to face themselves, see the incongruities between what they were and what they wanted to be, and decide that "enough is enough." They realized that they had no choice but to turn their lives around. And, what seems so remarkable and yet is not, they succeeded in finding their lost selves. It is not remarkable because we all have the capability of achieving that turnaround to authenticity and inner peace. Resilience is part and parcel of our constitutions; we just have to tap into it by believing in ourselves, others, and the spiritual power of the soul.

Like the phoenix from the ashes, we can return from near destruction to reawaken an authentic and vital sense of life.

Suggested Reading

Bradshaw, John. *Homecoming: Reclaiming and Championing Your Inner Child.* New York: Bantam Books, 1990.

Cohen, Alan. *The Dragon Doesn't Live Here Anymore.* San Diego: Alan Cohen Publications, 1988.

Kushner, Harold. *When Bad Things Happen to Good People.* New York: Avon Books, 1981.

_____. *When All You've Wanted Is Never Enough.* New York: Avon Books, 1981.

Levine, Saul. *Radical Departures.* New York: Harcourt Brace Jovanovich, 1984.

Peck, M. Scott. *The Road Less Traveled: A New Psychology of Love.* New York: Touchstone Books, 1978.

_____. *People of the Lie.* New York: Touchstone Books, 1985.

Schuller, Robert A. *The World's Greatest Comebacks.* Nashville, TN: Thomas A. Nelson, 1988.

Sheehy, Gail. *Passages.* New York: E.P. Dutton, 1974.

Stearns, Anne Kaiser. *Living Through Personal Crisis.* New York: Ballantine Books, 1985.

Trafford, Abigail. *Crazy Time: Surviving Divorce.* New York: Bantam Books, 1982.

Yalom, Irwin D. *Love's Executioner.* New York: Harper-Collins, 1989.

Saul Levine's previous books:

Radical Departures
Dear Doctor
Tell Me It's Only a Phase